This book is dedicated t(children Mark and Delia an could not have been possible without the urging, research and help of my daughter Delia, who also translated the many letters written by my mother.

Prologue

Friends have often asked how a quintessential Englishman could have such an odd name. I usually joke it off saying I'm a European mongrel. As a professor of chemistry, well known in the research field and having published many chemistry tomes it is actually quite useful to have a distinctive name. Now in my 80th year I have endeavoured to clarify my past, something I studiously avoided for the first three quarters of my life.

On 9th November 2015, my wife and I will be attending a memorial service in the town of Schwäbisch Gmünd in southern Germany. It happens to be the 77th anniversary of the awful night in 1938 when the Nazis smashed up Jewish homes, shops and synagogues and beat up and killed many Jews, sending thousands more to concentration camps. It is also a national Reconciliation Day in Germany. The particular reason for our visit is because my mother was born and raised in that town and ultimately died in a concentration camp.

Until relatively recently I have closed my mind to my turbulent past, particularly the first four years of my life in Germany, my family being permanently harassed and persecuted by the Nazis and several ending up in concentration camps. It took me many years to pluck up the courage to watch the film, Schindler's List, and tears streamed down my face. It was only the urging of my daughter Delia that finally made me look into my past of which I knew little. This book was put together as a result of several years of research by both Delia and myself. I now can visit all the places and sites in which my mother and her family and I suffered, without the deep-seated dread and bitterness that filled my mind in earlier years.

Otto Meth-Cohn, September 2015

Contents

Prologue 3

Chapter 1 Nearly German, nearly Jewish 6

Chapter 2 Nearly Scottish 22

Chapter 3 Nearly Christian 79

Chapter 4 Nearly Jewish – again 87

Chapter 5 Nearly a chemist 121

Chapter 6 Nearly a graduate, nearly a murderer 149

Chapter 7 Nearly a Christian graduate chemist 181

Chapter 8 Nearly a doctoral chemist 189

Chapter 9 Nearly Norwegian speaking 207

Chapter 10 Nearly converted to Norwegian living 221

Chapter 11 Nearly no longer nearly 225

Epilogue 230

Chapter 1

Nearly German, nearly Jewish

My mother, Dorothea Meth, always called Thea by family and friends, was born into a well-heeled, Jewish family in 1904 in Schwäbisch Gmünd, in the south-west of Germany, the third child of four. Her father, Alfred owned a thriving chain of stores, managed by various members of his wider family, all run to his strict routine. During the dark days of the Depression following WW1, Alfred had been a stalwart supporter of the local communities around his stores, helped by his wife Flora, known as Lori to the family. He left large heaps of coal outside his stores in winter for people to help themselves, ran a free food store for the poor and set up collections to support the people of Upper Silesia, where he and Lori were born. He was a respected and popular figure in the town and a pillar of the Jewish community and was a brilliant businessman.

As a newly married man in Königshutte, he plied his trade in household goods from a horse and cart. He made his name by always keeping his word to supply whatever people requested, even if he had not got the item in stock and even if it meant making a loss. He moved to southern Germany in 1901 as an apprentice to one of the clan of successful Jewish retailers from Silesia, opening his own store at 16 Bocksgasse – which shop is still there - in Schwäbisch Gmünd in 1903, where he and Lori lived above the store. Working hard was his style and soon he was employing the growing army of menfolk married to his wife's seven sisters. After a couple of years Alfred opened the Meth Department Store at 29 Bocksgasse and the family moved into a large villa, 90 (now 96) Oberbettringerstrasse with a governess and a chauffeur.

It was during the Depression that he developed a chain of low-price stores and, until Woolworths sued, branded them Wohlwert. Working with partners in Leipzig he had set up a joint purchasing scheme to cut the cost of their goods and sell everything at fixed prices, which proved highly successful. By 1932, Alfred was employing over 50 workers in several stores around southern Germany. The system had transformed the retail market but also upset the traditional retailers whose businesses were suffering as incomes fell.

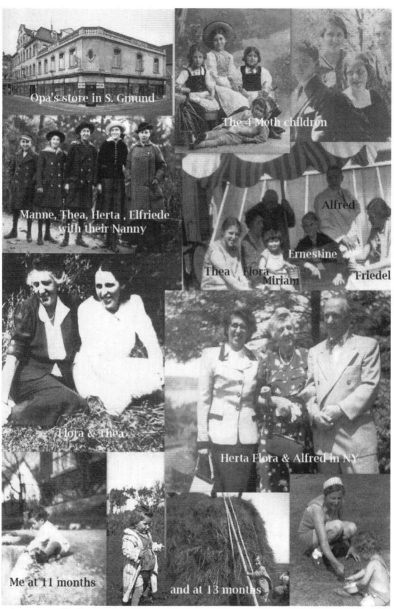

Opa's store in S. Gmund

The 4 Meth children

Manne, Thea, Herta , Elfriede with their Nanny

Alfred

Ernestine

Thea Flora
Miriam

Friedel

Flora & Thea

Herta Flora & Alfred in NY

Me at 11 months

and at 13 months

The Meth family

They blamed the hard-working and successful Jewish community for their woes and the Nazis quickly began to mobilise the angry retailers against the Jews. As soon as the Nazis took power in 1933, the stores came under attack and calls for boycotts began.

The pressure began to build. In the summer of 1934, Thea, who had trained as a social worker in a Jewish orphanage in Hamburg , decided to take a holiday. She went to the nearby Lake Constance, called Bodensee in German. Although we know very little of this momentous event in her life – and in mine – her friends say she met a student who was on a mountain hiking holiday there and fell in love. The relationship was doomed. He was not Jewish and that was bad enough for the Meths, but he was also a member of the Nazi brown shirt movement, the SA.

Despite their strict upbringing, only Friedl (the Schwäbisch custom of putting an 'l' after a name was a term of endearment which will be often seen in this book) , the oldest of Alfred and Lori's three daughters, led the respectable life expected of them. Thea's older sister Hertl had run off with her lover, Max Anguli (a Berlin tobacco seller who already had an illegitimate son) in the late 1920s and become pregnant. When Alfred found out, he had forced Max to marry her in a Czech registry office under his watchful eye. In 1931, Alfred set Max up as manager of a Wohlwert store in Ulm, bringing Hertl and their children back into the fold.

Thea, too, became pregnant, but whatever the real nature of the relationship there was no way she could envisage marriage. The Nuremberg Laws came out in 1935 making all relations between Jews and non-Jewish Germans illegal. She decided not to reveal his name to her family or friends and, with Hertl's help, she ran away to stay with a friend in The Hague, where she gave birth to me in the Emmaklinik on April 12, 1935. She gave me the name Ernst-Otto Meth – the first part of this unwieldy name was probably from her paternal grandmother, Ernestine, who had come with them to Germany and died in Stuttgart in the early 1940s. Was Otto my father's name? Intriguing! I am still searching for him.

Life was not going to be easy for an unmarried mother with a child of 'mixed' blood in an increasingly hostile world. Thea spent three months in The Hague, having registered my birth (amazingly, only recently I discovered through my daughter's efforts, that I had a Dutch birth certificate, though the father's name was, sadly, omitted).Then she decided it was time to move on. She had lived and worked all over Germany as a social worker and had many friends throughout the country. Her first move was probably to an old friend's town. It seems that returning home, which she had often done before during her itinerant working pattern, was too fraught with problems. She both wanted to protect the identity of her lover and not antagonise her parents any further.

8 weeks old in The Hague

...and a few months older

12 weeks old
Jena-Lobeda

6 months old in Jena

9 months old

September 1935 with Mutti Boock

Herrlingen 1938

Herrlingen spring 1939

26th June 1935
day before leaving
for UK

26th June 1935

Bodensee July 1938

Puppet show Herrlingen 1938

Early years

Thea next turned up in Jena. It seems probable that a friend she had worked with in Hamburg called Lissa Hartmann, who came from Jena, was the link. While in the Post Office there, she met and was befriended by a young mother, known to all as Mutti Boock, wife of a cobbler with 10 children of her own. She was invited to move in and this happy arrangement lasted for almost a year. Presumably in this time she maintained correspondence with her mother, though I imagine that it was some time before Alfred renewed contact with her.

Thea and I had an idyllic and sheltered life for those few short months. But Thea wanted to be back with her family. Life for Alfred and Lori was becoming increasingly problematic. The Nazi press had large banners 'Germans don't buy from Jews' and her father's store had a spy in next door's upper window, noting and reporting all who entered his store. Thea decided that the best option was to try and get a job in a children's home, finding eventually just such a position in Kathe Hamburg's children's home in Herrlingen, not far from Ulm.

Many years later, Mutti Boock, still living in Jena-Lobeda managed to trace me. After some letters, helpfully translated by one of her daughters, we were once more in touch. Clearly, she and Thea had had a marvellous and loving relationship and I was treated as a welcome addition to the large family. In 1973, I had an invitation to lecture in East German Universities (the Berlin Wall still dividing Germany) and accepted it with a view to visiting Mutti Boock and her husband. We struggled with my poor German but it is amazing how much we were able to discuss despite the problem. I returned a few years later, speaking at a large conference – in German – in Warnemunde, a Baltic resort. I will reveal more about these trips in a later chapter. Suffice to say I was again as warmly welcomed as at 12 weeks old.

In June 1936, while with Mutti Boock, Thea wrote to her sister Hertl '..... *Otto has his second back tooth (now he has 10 teeth). He is a lovely wild boy, a sweetie. He sends you his greetings ....*' Seven months later having moved to the children's home in Herrlingen near Ulm, she wrote ' ..... *I'm off to see my little boy. I'm looking forward to my beloved creature more than I can*

*say. When I got home yesterday they had cut off
my son's curls and sent my archangel away. Still,
he looks very nice and quite boyish......*

By 1936, the erstwhile close knit family was
rapidly breaking up. Hertl and her husband Max, a
keen Zionist, had left for Palestine in 1936. Max
invested the money he had managed to take out
of Germany in a promising ice factory in Haifa, but
they arrived just as the Arab Uprising erupted and
the factory was burnt down, leaving the family –
now with three children, Dina, Micha and Esther –
struggling to make ends meet.

Manne, the baby of the Meth family, born in
1906, had married a local girl, Anna Goldschmidt,
in 1931 and they lived in another impressive
mansion owned by his father at 63
Oberbettringerstrasse. They had a daughter, Dora,
two years later. Alfred set up Manne in nearby
Heilbronn as a partner in a Wohlwert store along
with a family friend, Max May. But Manne was
known more as a restless charmer than a hard
worker. Mr May had left for the USA days before
the Nazis came to power, but it was his wife who
took over the store. Manne left his family at the

house in Schwäbisch Gmünd and divorced Anna, who was, apparently, becoming increasingly mentally unstable. In 1936, he married Louisa Alzikiri, a Turkish Jewish woman he had met in Paris. They managed to get to Lisbon where Manne set up in business – finally finding his niche, as Thea commented in a letter to her father. He left Anna to look after Dora on her own in an increasingly hostile environment and the two narrowly escaped to New York in 1940 on the last boat out of Genoa. Getting them out was Anna's finest hour, her daughter Dora recalled. Meanwhile, Thea's oldest sister, Friedl, followed a more conventional route. She had married the cantor of Baden Baden synagogue, Max Grunfeld, and lived in the swish spa town with her two children, Miriam and Walter.

Alfred decided to sell his department store and villa in Schwäbisch Gmünd and join Friedl and Max in Baden Baden, a cosmopolitan city on the French border which had proved, so far, to be a haven of peace from Hitler's rabble-rousing activities. The arianisation sale of his store in 1936 was not advantageous, but sufficient to buy an imposing residence at 1 Kaiser Wilhelm Strasse, complete with servants and cooks.

Thea stayed in the Ulm area, where she got to know the local rabbi, Dr Julius Cohn. This warm-hearted man was actively keeping the Jewish community together in the face of growing persecution – holding classes for the young Jews who had been thrown out of school. But the health of his wife, Herta, was deteriorating. Thea went to visit him and found things far worse than she imagined. Herta was bed-ridden with cancer. She visited regularly over the coming months to help out as she could. Eventually she made a momentous decision. She offered to become his housekeeper and nurse his wife. At first she left me at the children's home, visiting regularly. Eventually, she decided that it would be easier to have me remain with her. The large, rambling house had plenty of space and Julius doted on me. Meanwhile, Herta was in terminal decline and died in February 1938. After a couple of months Thea resumed her position at the children's home in Herrlingen, where life was less fraught for a single mother and child.

In November 1938 Ulm experienced the extreme savagery of the Nazis. A bunch of local Nazi thugs marched into Ulm square, smashed windows of many of the Jewish houses and shops and continued to the synagogue which they set in flames. Thea watched in horror as Julius together with several colleagues were marched out into the square and made to walk in a circle around the fountain. As they walked they were beaten with rifle butts. Julius was the main target of their abuse and repeatedly dunked into the fountain until he almost drowned. This awful destruction and beating was repeated throughout Germany and Austria on the 9th and 10th November, many Jews being killed and up to 30,000 being dragged off to concentration camps. It became known as Kristallnacht. Poor Julius was in a very bad way and spent some time in hospital. On his return home, Thea had moved back in to care for him.

The horrors of Kristallnacht reverberated around the world. In Britain, a group made up of Quakers, Jewish leaders and other concerned groups urged the government to allow refugee children into the country. Acting quickly, the government decided to allow up to 10,000 children into Britain if their costs were underwritten. Before November was out, the BBC announced the need for foster families to take in refugees from Europe and a delegation of the new Refugee Children's Movement visited Germany to arrange transport and other logistics. The first refugees arrived in December 1938, from The Hook of Holland via Harwich and London Liverpool Street station.

Over the coming months Thea and Julius decided that the best way forward was to leave the country, not an easy prospect. They heard that married rabbis were being encouraged to leave Germany with their families but required a sponsor in the intended country of residence. After some writing, Julius discovered that the Jewish community of Edinburgh in Scotland were willing to take him in, but what about Thea and Otto? The apparent solution was for the rabbi to marry Thea, despite their 26 year age difference, which they did, with the blessing of the Ulm Jews in February 1939. In April 1939 Julius received permission to leave, no doubt salving the conscious of local government officials who colluded in his near murder. However, there was no mention of Thea in the leaving documents.

They decided that he should go and she would do her best to follow, thinking it was a mere glitch in the bureaucracy. Still in very poor health, Julius gave his last sermon in April 1939 and left in early May.

Thea was in a quandary. She was in demand both at the Herrlingen children's home and in a nearby old people's home that was without staff. So many Jews had left or been uprooted. She had a young son, a distraught mother, an estranged and suffering father and now also, a distant husband in poor health. Her attempts to leave Germany were met with red tape problems but she discovered that a Quaker organisation in England had organised a ship to sail from The Hook of Holland to Harwich in England in June. Surprisingly, she received acceptance quickly for me to be one of them, hoping to follow in due course. On June 26th 1939, she escorted me, aged 4, to Ulm station, armed with a tiny suitcase with a change of clothes made by herself and a little food for the journey. Older children lifted me onto the train, crowded with happy, sad, weeping, cheering, young and older children, marshalled by officious guards and military personnel, off to an unknown future.

A distraught Thea went straight back to Herrlingen and took up the post as deputy head of the Jewish old people's home.

Chapter 2

Nearly Scottish

Arriving at Harwich on 27th June, the well organised volunteers met the children as they disembarked, sorted them out and fixed them up with Landing Certificates – many, including myself having no Birth Certificates but others having a German registration document – and linked them up as quickly as possible into their groups for their further travels. Most of the children were put on the awaiting train that took them to London, Liverpool Street. Here they were met with their foster family or a person to take them on to them. Bewildered children found that their German language – or in some cases Czechoslovakian or Polish – met with blank stares, but the new sights and friendly faces was a pleasant change from the officious German authorities that they had been faced with in the past.

I was met by a particularly friendly lady who seemed excellent at making herself understood with gestures, smiles and words that, although meaningless, conveyed her intentions. Holding my hand she escorted me through the throng of children and adults, through the station and onto a most strange, red bus. The busy London scenes were amazing to my unfamiliar eyes, buses and taxis, horses and carts, large impressive buildings and strange shaped churches with high steeples and more people than I'd ever seen before. I stayed in a large house for a few days with several other German children and was fed as if I hadn't eaten for weeks. Then a lady arrived and took me on another of those intriguing red buses.

Arriving at Kings Cross station we were soon on a train to Edinburgh. The lady kept pointing to herself and saying 'Armyne' and to me saying 'Otto'. So very soon I picked up her name, was able to tell her that I needed the toilet and that I enjoyed the apple and rough wholemeal cheese sandwiches that she had brought. Already my English vocabulary was growing with 'Sankyou', 'pleese' and some funny words when I pointed out of the window at a passing curiosity. 'Edinbu' proved a problem but I obviously had the Peter Sellers type of mimic-mind and by the time we arrived in Edinburgh I had some smattering of very basic English.

We arrived in Edinburgh after I had fallen asleep for most of the journey and walked the long trek to Upper Dean Terrace. I refuse to be carried up the hill and clung to my little case, not knowing what was inside it. On arrival the door was flung open by a little chubby boy with no clothes on, Charles, who said nothing but just stared as his little sister, Gillian, similarly unclad, came running up and babbled eagerly to me. Armyne encouraged me in and after long silences, slowly Charles brought out some toys, Gill continued to babble, calling me Otty. Soon curiosity overtook our uncertainties and we were playing together. I would say sankyou to Charles, which brought howls of laughter.

Armyne kept a diary of the first few months after my arrival. She began on Sunday July 2nd: *'Otto Cohn, a 4 year old refugee kid arrived from Germany on Friday night. His mother, poor soul, is still there. If he knew English it would be easy to distract his attention as he has a good sense of humour. He manages wonderfully well in spite of language questions. It's like handling Gillian, who being 18 months old, knows a few words – but it is Gill with a 4 year old mentality.*

Otto is a wild little creature. Though very thin and small and under-nourished he is 6 months older than Charles, who is much bigger all round.'

July 3rd: *'A friend brought their Austrian refugee girl to tea yesterday. Otto enjoyed it but was a little upset going to bed. ..... Otto gets into rages when he kicks and bites. One has to be a bit firm with him and it is difficult having no common language. He has got an awfully sweet side to him though, and I'm very fond of the wee creature.'*

The few, smart terraced houses on Upper Dean Terrace had a communal walled garden of several acres which one entered with a key, sloping down to the Waters-of-Leith. We were often allowed to play there unsupervised, quite safely despite the water and lots of trees to climb. On July 7th Armyne wrote *'This afternoon I joined Otto & Charles in the garden after tea. They immediately started to fight, I being the bone of contention, and Charles behaved very badly. I carried him off crying and struggling, telling him that if he does such silly babyish things as to hit etc. he must be treated like a baby. I took him to a distant seat and had a long talk with him and explained that men didn't go around hitting each other(!) and that he must be kind to Otto. He listened very quietly. ... I told him he must be nice to Otto then he would be nice to him. .... When we got home the two started to squabble over some toys and Otto was about to bite Charles when I shouted as loudly as I could "No Otto!" He looked astonished and then began to cry. I took him on my knee and told him he must never do that. I think it got through to him. I told Charles to give Otto the toy and a few minutes later Otto gave it back to him. They kept giving things to each other and played very peaceably together. I told them they were very good and praised and kissed them both and Charles went to bed in a very happy state. I feel this may have done a little good. Otto is a very intelligent little creature and I think they must both learn that fighting is just NOT DONE otherwise they will both be unhappy. I have affection for Otto. There is good stuff in him. We will see how things work out.'*

The Ware family, Harry and Armyne, were both artists of some ability, both exhibiting paintings and etchings in the Royal Scottish Academy and the National Gallery of Scotland and Harry was the art teacher at nearby Fettes College. They were Nature Cure believers, strict vegetarians and who drank no tea or coffee and took no medicines. When ill, they fasted till better – or dead. Only wholemeal bread, home-made, was eaten with plentiful cheese, fruit and vegetables, often raw. Colds were treated by cutting out bread mostly. Despite their beliefs Harry enjoyed his pipe, believed in spitting – into a spittoon, apparently – and scolded me for spitting on the bare wooden floor. He told me I could spit into the cast iron stove, lifting the lid! We children tended to wear very little most of the time, indoors and out. He was very popular as a teacher with his pupils if not the other staff, who thought him an odd character and was also popular in the community, where they were considered rather Bohemian.

A week after my arrival Armyne wrote: *'Yesterday was a very satisfactory day with the children. Today things are going so much better. They play with each other without fighting and are becoming much more friendly. While I was bathing Gill, Harry and Charles were washing up. Otto came into the kitchen and wanted to help too. There was a frightful shindig and they started to hit each other. Harry sent Otto out of the room – he was the aggressor –and when he came back they took turns in doing the washing and drying up with perfect quietness and amicability. This is a huge step. There has been no biting or kicking, only a little quite friendly puppy fighting occasionally. The two little boys are dancing around the room, hand in hand, to the gramophone. Otto's little eyes are losing their rather beady, fierce look and he is much happier. He sees that we are perfectly fair. Charles, for instance, was sent out of the room for another offence during the afternoon.'*

Both Harry and Armyne were children of high ranking military folk. Harry's father was already a famous figure, Major General Sir Fabian Ware, the man responsible for creating the Commonwealth War Graves Commission during the First World War, being too old to join up, and he continued this work in the Second World War under the patronage of Winston Churchill. Although never an army man, he was given the appropriate rank to allow his war work. To us he was 'Pewg' and his wife was 'Wa', why I don't know. He lived in a large house and grounds in the Cotswold village of

Amberley and his close friends included many in the upper ranks of society. While supporters of the arts, his mother was only willing to accept him as an artist if he became an establishment figure as an artist of fame. Armyne was the daughter of a Scottish Lieutenant Colonel who made his name in India and retired to Aboyne, Aberdeenshire.

On July 12th she continued: *'Little Otto is a reformed character! He and Charles get on splendidly now. If either of them are silly and seriously attack the other they leave the room and when they return the game goes on without any trouble. Otto eats his food well and is no trouble.* .... and on the 14th July: *'Otto's step-father, Julius, came to tea yesterday. I don't think he upset the child much but 'grown ups' are curious. He asked if he should talk to Otto about his home; we said we thought it would better not to, but he couldn't resist mentioning 'Thea' to see what affect it had on Otto. They* <u>will</u> *think of themselves and not the children! Luckily, I don't think Otto heard.*

Poor wee Otto – he is a dear wee soul and very affectionate. Last night when I came down from saying goodnight to Charles I heard 'Armyne' and went into Otto's room, finding him quite happy but wanting to be tucked up. He needs a great deal of love. I think a good feeding and getting his little body healthy and strong should make a fine person of him.'

Reading other topics in her diary, which seems to have been terminated by the onset of war and their personal tribulations arising therefrom, she was a very moral, selfless, thinking and loving person. She and Harry had an interesting relationship in which they often discussed marriage, children and life in a surprisingly philosophical manner. They took us on long walks in the country, introduced us to everything to do with nature and much of that knowledge and interest persists to this day. We would go foraging for all nature's bounty, returning with full bags and often covered in scratches, but happy. Blackberry pie with custard was always a favourite. It only dawned on me much later in life, why I seemed instinctively to know the names of birds and flowers, insects and trees. Harry held strong and radical views on most subjects. They were both horrified by the rapidly developing talk of war and Harry was determined that in no way would he join the armed forces. His upbringing in a household totally driven by the effects of war had convinced him of the pointlessness of fighting wars. However, Hitler and his Nazi party were becoming ever more strident and determined to overrun Europe. The future certainly looked bleak. Harry kept himself busy painting, gardening and walking, with nature as his teacher – and burying his head in the sand regarding the war.

Meanwhile, in Baden Baden the Meth family were daily witnessing the extreme anti-Semitism all around them. Even buying essentials was a daily painful experience of running the gauntlet. People they had previously regarded as reasonable neighbours would either shun them or worse. Daily life as a Jew was becoming a battle. Thea similarly was experiencing problems in trying to feed and care for elderly and infirm Jewish residents of the care home. Many of the old men had fought in the first world war for Germany, had suffered in the appalling aftermath of the great Depression of the '20s, some having been shopkeepers trying to keep their communities supplied. They remembered when everything was 'erzatz' – substituted – so that ground acorns replaced coffee, paper underwear, paper Mark notes instead of metal etc. They recalled when inflation resulted in million and even trillion Mark notes. They were perplexed that they were now regarded with loathing.

Back in Edinburgh, Armyne records on 22nd July that *'Harry took 40 boys from Fettes on a Natural History Expedition after lunch. Luckily, the weather down at Hailes Castle near Haddington* (a 14th century castle and estate several miles east of Edinburgh) *was better than here and it was a huge success. I had a fairly hectic day with the three kids. It was too wet to go out and they were pretty good most of the time. – painted a lot of pictures, listened to the gramophone and had some splendid rough and tumbles, with Gill enjoying it as much as the boys. She's quite a tom-boy.*

Charles is much more on top of things and less of a cry-baby. It is good for him to realise at an early age that everything does not belong to him. Mrs Thomson said on the phone to Harry that it was very hard on Charles having another child in the house, but I didn't agree. I notice how much brighter and naughtier (I mean in a nice way) he is. He and Otto tease me tremendously and simply shriek with laughter and it is so much better for Charles not to live only with grown-ups. He isn't a bit jealous of Otto with Harry and me. I feel that the fact that he doesn't sleep with Otto is a great thing. They aren't too much on top of each other.'

A few days later she records *'The relationship between Charles and Otto is almost perfect now. They hardly ever fight seriously and play most happily together.*

Otto spent the day with Julius yesterday, who took him to the zoo – but he came home quite happily to us and it does not appear to have upset him at all.'

July 29th: *'The children really seem to have settled down. Neither bully the other much now and Gill is very fond of Otto whom she calls Otty. She is a delightful creature. We took them to Hopetoun (a 17th century stately home near Edinburgh) yesterday for their tea and they were just like three puppies tumbling about in the long grass and picking flowers. All most amicable. Otto is looking much fatter and has a good colour.'*

It wasn't always quite so rosy in the Ware house. It seems that within a month I was speaking fluently in English and totally integrated in living in this new environment! Children are so adaptable. Not surprisingly there were also bad days. On August 6th Armyne wrote: *'Rather a difficult day with the children – chiefly because we were both rather tired and cross ourselves. One's own frame of mind can so quickly react upon them. Harry had them in the garden in the afternoon while I got their tea ready; he reported that they were odious.*

However, the next day was better: *'The children behaved splendidly this afternoon. I'm so happy about it. Once again, it is one's own attitude which means everything. It's almost uncanny how it comes in again and again. Love is the one magic that can really change the world. I think that this time with Otto and Charles has taught me something that I always refused to believe and that it has been an invaluable lesson......'*

The last entry I have is on 19th August when she notes that *'Otto and Charles are getting on well together now. Otto spent time with Julius yesterday and greeted Harry with shouts of glee when he came to collect him. He is really happy here and is a different boy.'* Julius never recovered from his treatment by the Nazis and sadly he survived for only 9 months in Britain, dying at the house of Dora, Flora's sister, in London.

Time was spent with Armyne's parents in Aboyne for two weeks in September though I have no record, apart from a few photographs, that suggest we children had a whale of a time together. On September 1st Hitler began the invasion of Poland; Britain and France declared war on Germany two days later. Harry had declared himself a conscientious objector and signed up for forestry duties. He was immediately regarded as unpatriotic and a coward by some. No doubt his father had some influence in his first job as a forester as he was transferred to the Cotswolds.

We all moved to live in the small cottage in the large grounds of Sir Fabian's house in Amberley not far from Stroud. This delightful village is now owned by the National Trust and has hardly changed since our time there. Picturesque houses in Cotswold stone are built around an undulating common, used by all the community for grazing, play, horse riding, golf and other activities, often all at the same time! We children loved it and had the occasional special tea with 'Wa' and occasionally 'Pewg' when he was at home. Important visitors were aplenty but to us children they were just boring adults. I was briefly an object of curiosity. Charles, Gill and I were happy in the new environment despite the upheaval and life continued – much in the nude – as before. Harry grew vegetables and Charlie and I enjoyed working in the garden. I especially enjoyed sawing wood for the wood-burning pot stove and apparently was quite good at it! No Health & Safety issues then. I can recall enjoying bowling hoops with the children on the common. On another occasion I remember the three of us were sat on a wall – no clothes on – and Gill fell backwards into some nettles. Not only was I horrified at the screaming, red-blotched Gill, but I was blamed for pushing her off (not surprisingly, Gill also remembered that occasion when we met over 60 years later). Happy days ..... A few months after arriving in Amberley, the Wares heard that Julius had died. While this was very sad, it was not an issue in my young mind. Charlie and I were enrolled at an interesting school nearby not long after our arrival. The pupils and staff from The Mount School in Mill Hill, London (now a rather smart, independent fee-paying school for girls) had been evacuated to the Cotswolds and we were allowed to join them! My first report at the end of term, 29th July 1941, had some interesting comments.

Reading – Works very hard, if spasmodically

Writing – Has made great efforts to improve

Numbers – Good, shows keen interest, considerable aptitude

Nature study – Good, shows keen interest and has good memory

Music – Shows extremely keen rhythmic sense

Form mistress report: Otto has shown a real keenness for work though must try to be more independent. He is improving in his attitude towards other children though still rather intolerant; inclined to be rough and to show off.

I note much from the Wares upbringing had rubbed off! Armyne's diary often became remarkably philosophical. *'Harry & I walked to the other end of Corstorphine Hill* (a fine, woody walk on one of Edinburgh's seven hills) *and back this morning. We came to the conclusion that one of the causes of trouble in married life is the identification of the wife with the mother in a man's mind – that is if he has not got on well with his mother. He is apt to foist his mother's faults on his wife in addition to her own! Poor mothers! They have a hard time of it at the hands of psychologists. It seems impossible for them to do right. If anyone has the need to be 'non-attached' it is a mother. As a matter of fact I feel pretty non-attached to both the children – that is I love them dearly but as far as I can make out I have very little 'possessive' love for them. I feel that they are darlings but not MY darlings. I was much struck with this fact when Charles was born – there he lay in the cot by my bed – a lovely fawn-like creature, so separate – such a complete* <u>individual</u>. *Except that he was formed within me and fed by me, he seemed to have nothing to do with me. I was there to give him food, love and warmth and to spend my life doing the best I could for him, but I felt then and always will that I could never call him mine. In some ways the feeling I have for little Otto is nearly the same as I have for Charles and Gillian..... I do feel the same warmth when I look at his dear little face and see that heart-breaking fragility, trust and confidence that a grown up can always put things right. If we could only retain that non-attachment with our lovers which we have with our children, marriage would be a different thing. We don't love the other enough – we love ourselves too much. Real love must be selfless..... True love must be constant I think, and free, and above all generous.*

What a remarkable lady and mother.

Life continued pleasantly for us children despite the war, privations and the little money coming in from Harry's forestry and the stigma he had to endure. After two years based in the Cotswolds, Harry was eventually posted to Coniston in the Lake District – accommodation being in a shepherd's cottage with very limited space and facilities. Before that time he had a precarious and mobile existence and I only added to his problems. Crunch time had come. While Armyne was willing to continue keeping 3 children, Harry was now implacable that the time had come that they move me on. At the best of times it was a struggle, especially given their vegetarian lifestyle; now it was becoming impossible for him. They came to the decision to approach the National Children's Home organisation. They were sent a long questionnaire with most questions regarding family background and birth certificate being left blank. They even inquired regarding any workhouse spells or mental and physical defects in the family. Furthermore, I was given a medical examination which indicated that I needed my tonsils removing – I can clearly remember the awful pain of the event which took place some months later. Harry decided to write his own response rather than handle this bureaucratic drivel. Eventually, they agreed to take on this German refugee, but not without some serious concerns. To put them fully in the picture, on the 22nd September 1941 he wrote to their headquarters as follows:

'I think I better give you a few notes about the food, health treatment and so on that we have

given Otto for the last two years. We realise that those responsible for him will naturally wish to bring him up in their own way, but we would like to point out that any sudden drastic change in his food or giving him medicine, to which he is entirely unused (he has had no medicine or injections or anything of that kind since he has been with us) might have serious results.... We have always been in the habit of living on the food reform lines, which of course, more and more people are doing now, in fact are bound to under wartime conditions. Otto has never eaten meat, fish or fowl and has the vegetarian cheese ration. But a gradual change to a flesh diet would do him no harm as long as he keeps to plenty of vegetables, especially raw salads. In winter, he is very fond of grated carrot or raw shredded cabbage. We are very keen on wholemeal bread and of course no tea, coffee or anything like that. He was a miserable specimen when he first came to us and has improved in health and energy enormously on the diet.

With regards to medicines and injections we are patients of Nature Cure practitioners, who are opposed to such things. Whenever he is ill we fast him and keep him off too much bread and starchy food if he has a cold. He is a very healthy child and I don't think you will find him difficult in health matters. Regarding psychological matters, Dr Hills of Stroud, a child psychologist has pronounced him perfectly normal………………

We have brought him up to work in the house with our own children and he is always willing to wash up and so on. He and my small son love working in the garden and are really good at the job! He is also good with a saw and has helped cut a lot of our wood. As my job at the moment is wood-cutting I can speak with some professional knowledge. If you ever find him with nothing to do, or in any way bored, he will always love work of this sort………….

……… we would always welcome news of him regularly and if he ever got very keen to pay us a visit …. we should be delighted to have him for a period. …….

He also suggested that I was very excited about the idea of a new home with lots of children – which I very much doubt.

The removal date for the Wares arrived in late September 1941 with still no resolution to my domicile and a hasty decision by the NCH was to house me temporarily in a home of theirs in 50 Romola Road, London SE24 – slap in the bombing heart of Britain. I was there for 3 months and have absolutely no memory of the stay whatever. I'm fairly certain that I was deeply unhappy and very confused. I probably attended the local school – and often the air raid shelter.

Further form filling on my behalf, which indicated that I was generally in sound health, having suffered from measles and whooping cough, had swollen tonsils and was prone to bed-wetting. Surprise, surprise. A comment indicated that: *'his bed-wetting could be quickly solved under strict supervision.'* Hmmm …..

…. and so to Princess Alice Orphanage, Sutton Coldfield, Birmingham.

But before we go there I need to remind readers of the problems at the German end. On the 22nd October 1940, Alfred and Flora were deported to southern France, then under the Vichy government, together with 6,500 other Jews from

Baden Baden and the surroundings. (The Vichy government had signed an armistice with the Nazis.) They were stripped of their citizenship and having no advanced warning, could take hardly any luggage and the equivalent of $50 in cash. Their entire belongings and wealth were confiscated by the state. They were transported to the concentration camp of Gurs on the Spanish border, near Pau. This dilapidated camp remained from the Spanish civil war days, when Spaniards escaping Franco were detained there. There was no furniture, but a few bedframes and limited blankets and eating utensils, food often eaten directly from cans. 382 flimsy cabins covered the site.

One inmate wrote 'The barracks are dark, without daylight, there being no windows. We squat on a layer of straw on dirty floors. Hunger governs our feelings. Misery, homesickness and hopelessness destroy us. Watery soup twice a day with a little bread is our portion. Old people up to 100 years of age, invalids, blind, paralysed, deaf-mutes, children and babies all had to take this dreadful journey. A convict sentenced to death knows how long he has to suffer. We don't know whether or when the gates of freedom and humanity will ever open to us again.'

More than 1000 died of malnutrition, typhus or dysentery. The Swiss Red Cross and Quakers helped out with medicines and food supplements and the mortality decreased. Some of the Jewish children were taken into French homes to save them from the Gestapo. Alfred was part of a gang made to work with a French farmer, which probably helped him and Flora to survive. Apparently the deportation of Jews from Baden Baden area was the first in Adolf Eichmann's plan to remove all Jews from Germany. Meanwhile, Alfred's Ulm cinema had become the 'confirmation' equivalent for young Nazis, where 'youth consecrations' were held every Sunday.

Thea was a great letter-writer, though invariably she wrote in haste in difficult-to-read old German script. Some of her letters were kept by her sister Herta and have been translated by my very patient daughter. They are very informative and moving and continued for several years, even through the war.

On 2nd June 1939, after Julius had left for Edinburgh but before she sent me to the UK she wrote to her sister Frieda, who was staying in Strasbourg, France *'My good sister, Are you alone in France? Your husband is working. I am not alone here for a change. It's very nice. I'm learning English with Uncle …. We're learning from the book I wanted to send you. I guess you are learning French now? I'm going back on Monday and must get things packed. Julius writes good things about Edinburgh. I'm so glad that he's been accepted so well and treated kindly everywhere; it's very fortunate for us.'*

By the end of 1940, Thea had become head of the old people's home in Heilbronn-Sontheim, set up in the house of Dr Julius Picard, 12 Lauffenstrasse. Dr Picard was an incredibly popular and able doctor to the community. Although he was not Jewish, his wife Gertrude was and he stood by her during all the persecution from Kristallnacht onwards. On that fateful night her synagogue was destroyed and they were both badly beaten up and left for dead. Their neighbours came every night when the Nazi guards were off duty and cared for them. His two sons were also medical doctors and had emigrated to USA in 1936 and 1937. Despite incredible harassment, and still suffering from their traumas, they managed to escape to the USA via Portugal. To pay for the travel they sold their furniture – secretly at night – to their neighbours. Throughout this time Thea kept in touch with her family and friends. In particular, she used a friend, Dr Schmal in St Gallen, Switzerland as a conduit to keep in touch. It appears she was also in touch with the Wares, directly or indirectly, and knew of my living with them and eventually leaving them. She made strenuous efforts to obtain a visa to emigrate to the USA, who were then not in the war, sadly without success.

Heilbronn area had a long history of rampant anti-Semitism, coming to a head on Kristallnacht, though all Polish Jews in the town had been deported and dumped on the Polish border several months earlier.

The house in Heilbronn put up about 22 elderly and sick patients and the staff included a Doctor Essinger and two assistant nurses. Despite unbelievable hardships, Thea managed to continue running this home until on 20th August 1942, when she and 22 old people were transported via Stuttgart on the last deportation from the town, number 848, to the concentration camp of Theresienstadt in Czechoslovakia. This was the final removal of Jews from Württemberg.

It seems evident that Thea both loved the work and was much appreciated by the residents.

In May 1941 she wrote a long letter to her parents, incarcerated in the Gur concentration camp, which reveals much of the conditions and the endeavours of Thea to hold the family together despite all:

My dear loves,

I have such a terrible conscience when I think about you. I've not written for ages. And how many lovely messages have I had from you in the meantime. Well, there's been so much work since Easter Sunday when I last wrote. In fact quite a lot has changed since then as I mentioned in my last letter. Our residents have moved in. First there were 8, two couples, a widow and three spinsters. Another 4 are due to come. I have to say some of them are really nice people, particularly one couple, who help out a lot despite their age, so really are a comfort to me. I've also been lucky in getting help – a widow, the sister-in-law of Henls from Heilbronn, has registered to help out for 6 weeks. She managed a restaurant for 22 years that was famous for its roast goose and other goose dishes. She cooks really wonderfully and has taken over the kitchen. Everything she puts on the table tastes really first class. And she is very hardworking and independent and takes a lot of work off my shoulders. But you can imagine that in an organisation with 12 residents, some of whom are really ill and bedridden, there is a lot of work and I don't get much peace all day. But I keep telling myself I really am very happy at work. I look after the house, do the shopping, look after the patients etc. Workers come or don't come, the telephone rings, there are letters to write, then I help out a bit in the kitchen, wash the dishes too. We do a weekly wash and so it goes on. We have very strict austerity measures – the cost per person per day is not allowed to be more than 75 pfennig. We also get no help except for the wash. I'm hoping that the women from the Kille (?) will help me out with the cleaning every now and then so I'm not left with everything. The residents are supposed to help but most of them are too fragile and can't do much.

I told you the house is a little like the one in the Bettringerstrasse, two floors. I have a lovely big room on the first floor that is also my office and is really airy and beautiful. There is a very big garden, with fruit trees and vegetables and we work very hard there. Soon we will have our own salad. It's really a lovely place, hopefully we'll be allowed to remain here for some time..

So I've talked enough about me and you are up to date on what I'm doing and how I am. Now I want to answer your letters one by one. So you were really busy and wrote on 16.4, 23.4 and 28.4. What really pleased me was that Friedel and Max were able to visit you and Friedel's positive report calmed me down and made me very happy. It's really such a silver lining that Fridele who is so good and always soldiers on, is so close to you and that you can get together. That really pleases me and is such a comfort to the whole family. Now you can draw on that memory and all that is so *difficult is easier to bear when you have the chance to talk with your nearest and dearest. It's so good that Friedel has put on a bit of weight. We really have to thank God for his mercy in keeping you all healthy and guiding you so far. Don't give in to mourning about what you have lost even though I can understand that so well. But we see time and again nowadays that property is just foam, with no guarantee. If you can hold on to life and keep up your courage and hold on to your health, then it is all worthwhile. And I don't find it bad that you have to take from other people. Throughout your life you have always been doing good for other people and now the shoe is on the other foot. That's OK so I want to urge you to accept clothes from Arnold or have some sent over. The post often takes longer than you think so maybe these things could be useful. Mr May* (an old partner of Alfred who had escaped to USA) *will work for you there I'm convinced of it; he has proved to be a very loyal friend and we all owe him a debt of gratitude, as also Uncle Ludwig to whom I send warm greetings. I have already asked whether you think it would be right for me to visit Mrs May* (who remained in Germany running the family business) – *I don't want to do it until I hear from.*

Now I will answer your questions one by one. I can only use one piece of paper because I have to included other letters with this one.

I was really upset with Aunt Emma that she let you know the bad news but I'm afraid it's true. But Aunt Emma is trying to get some of your money out, maybe she will be able to - I do hope so. You don't need to worry about what she'll live on – so far she's always had sufficient until now and she hasn't suffered. Mrs Keiles also sent me 50. Gugges behaved very badly – a poor friend in a time of need and I recall, my dear father, what you told me about him. He's now gone. I got 100 from him once and then just excuses and denials. In the end I didn't turn to him any more and let it go. Lotte met him one time in the street and told him that Alfred and Lori (Thea's parents) *had been deported. If that made any impression on him, he could have done the same, but he didn't. Did he visit Manner? By the way, Manner wrote me a nice letter and said he had sent a package but that it hasn't arrived yet. Gromele* (Thea's paternal grandmother) *and I got something from his account. I am really happy that he also has a job now. He sounds happy. You will also have got news from the Ismars, who have written to you often. They recently wrote to say that uncle starts work at a wood-processing factory on the 15th of this month. I sent him on a letter from Klare and wrote in a few words – he replied today. Two weeks before I had asked him to be a sponsor for me* (for emigration purposes) *but he didn't mention it at all. I wonder whether he got my first letter? It is really so important for me. I'll send him a copy of it. He says he is doing everything he can for the relatives but he is not a wealthy man and his liabilities are continually increasing.*

I have heard nothing about Ottole and his further journeys; I was asked to provide the names of relatives in the USA, but I can't really put down uncle Siegar (Alfred's brother)*.*

By the way, the papers arrived well – thanks a lot for them. Our friend Mr May sent them which amazed me. I also got the letter from Anna Gronich and was really pleased about that. How terrible that she is also there with you. She writes so kindly and I really thank her for remembering me. Julius loved this sister of his very much. Please thank her very much from me. I won't have time to write in the next few days.

Now, finally, I want to congratulate you father on your birthday. I hope the post hurries up and brings you my warmest greetings and wishes on time and not too belatedly. Dear father, I just want to wish you that this hardest year of your life is now well and truly over and that things improve for you, my loves. And that God enables you to hold on to your love for life, your health and your courageous partner for many, many years. And that we all will see each other again in peace and joy! And now I'll let this letter find its way to you. I hope it finds you in good health and I greet you thousands of times from the bottom of my heart,

Your daughter Tea

Please greet Friedele and Max too.

On the 21st August 1941 she wrote to the family via Dr Schmal

……. So my lovely ones, I'm back home again. I came back yesterday evening after being with the Persis family ……. All of them send their best greetings, including Marianne who I could only speak to by phone. I think the Persis's were really happy I came and they looked after me well………

On my return I was greeted with such a celebration here, you can't imagine – lots of flowers everywhere, someone recited a poem and lots of joy everywhere. You would have been so happy if you had seen it – how nice it all was. It was evident how much they all appreciate me and rely on me. All of them, the men and the women, have worked so wonderfully in the house and the garden, for example making a garden shed out of bits and pieces and clearing a large piece of land for growing things etc. This morning they showed me everything with such pride before breakfast. My assistants managed everything very well; everything went smoothly and was managed just as I wanted…..

She wrote another letter to her brother Manne in December 1941

.... *I'm writing to you today because yesterday I got a bill from Barr Muring for the first time in ages concerning my attempts to emigrate. It is calculated for half a year – for the time from 1.7-1.12 1941 and amounting to RM 248.60. What do you think about that? I almost 'fell on my arse' Manne. There's no way I can afford that amount. I would need around 8 months to earn that. Just think: I earn RM50, 20 go to Gromele,* (her grandmother, Ernestine) *that leaves 30. I'm not in need and I can easily get by and I still have emergency savings. But what can we do? We'll certainly have to pay the bill. I think once you're in the USA you would have the chance to get it sent over. It could be useful for you. Please let me know as soon as possible. I also want to ask Dr Ostertag to transfer some money from your current account. What do you think Mannlein – could you ask him to do that? By the way, I was really happy to get your package with honey – I sent it straight on to Vienna. Thanks a lot. Could you think, my lovely brother, about sending some coffee – I have almost none left and every now and then it really perks me up.*

So now my day is over. Being ill, I haven't worked much – just let the others work for me. This afternoon I was taken to Heilbronn. Dr Essinger had invited me for tea and after tea he burnt the carbuncle out of my right cheek that I, pig that I am, had managed to become more serious by messing around with it. The operation was successful and I'm still alive. He anaesthetised me beforehand. The doctor is really nice and we are close – but he is not going to be a son-in-law ....

So – I'm off to bed and that's it for today. I'm really living very sensibly just as you like it. Greetings and kisses to you all.

Your Tea

On the 11ᵗʰ February 1942, after a long and bitterly cold winter she wrote to Dr Schmal *'Dear Uncle Schmal, Thank you very much for the letter of 1ˢᵗ January which I received yesterday (!) and which I had been waiting for with such longing. It's sad that Alfred and Flora [*her parents – in Gur concentration camp*] are so unwilling to reconsider and I can quite believe that in their* *hearts they sometimes just want to give up working. Is Flora better off staying with Alfred? How is the food situation there? It's so sad that one is unable to help. I would so much like to do something but I can't, my hands are tied. I can't even send post, though I was able to send one package. I'm glad that little Otto managed to find a place to live with other people. Is that the same place that he was in the first time?* (I had been transferred to the Birmingham orphanage and she refers to the brief London sojourn) *I recently received news from Mrs Ware on 9th February saying how well he was doing. Still, I'm not worried. I have lots of work, am healthy and in good spirits. I hope the same goes for you.'*

On 13th February 1942 she wrote to her brother Manne, who had escaped to Lisbon, Portugal *'I've had to use you as a 'Postillion d'amour' to tell Alfred and Flora that I received their letter of 15th January and was very glad finally to get news, even if it wasn't so good. Better any news than none. I recently received a letter from Mr Lang, a child of one of my patients. They were recently in Gurs and wrote enthusiastically from Casablanca. I really wish you could take our parents to Casablanca. ….*

We have so much work because one of my girls is ill, as is Dr Essinger, and as a result I have no time to write.'

A couple of weeks later she wrote further to the family via Manne:

My dearest brother and parents,

I have been dying to write this letter to you for ages, I can tell you. It's really awful when you just don't ever get a chance to write. You keep putting it off from one day to the next and then every evening you're unhappy because you go to bed with unfinished business. I have at least managed to shoot off a few postcards to you in the meantime to let you know I'm fine. Now it's Sunday afternoon, I'm off duty and very glad to have time to myself again after a week full of hard work. And now I can finally get a letter off to you.

I got your lovely letters from December and January. It is indeed very sad that you are no closer to your destination. But I think you really mustn't give up hope. Your good natures will let you overcome all the difficulties, shortages, disappointments and one day you will be able to reach the destination you are longing for. It is still better that you are there even if it is sometimes difficult to live under such circumstances. You really haven't deserved this but it won't remain this way. Just look at Kaethe and Josef who have it so much harder than you. I wrote to you already that they are in Lo., where Richard Faerber was during the war. I haven't had news from them directly, I've sent money but there is no post service at present. We've also heard nothing from Lotte and the others. We've written but we don't know if they received anything. By the way, do you know the address of Lotte's sister? Are you in contact with her, my dear mother? She would be very interested, maybe she hasn't heard of the change. Lotte is working there as a carer and I hope that the work is at least a bearable. Sister Erna is also there. Maybe the work is good for Lotte, that's also possible. Her mother and aunt will very soon be taken into a residential home that is being set up next to Julius's last home Ulm. These kind of residential and old-people's homes are being set up in several places in the countryside and all the people are being moved there from the towns. I do hope that we'll be able to stay a long time but even if there is a change I'm not worried because there will always be enough work for me. I know that I am popular and well regarded in the central organisation and that makes it easier to be calm about the future.

I've got to tell you now about Dr. Essinger since you've asked about him a few times. We're very good friends and are really very close. He is such a clever, fine, reliable and good person and I know no one who I would rather have as a co-worker and friend. But he suffers from serious heart disease and he has too great a sense of responsibility to bind my life to his under the present circumstances. That's why you mustn't get your hopes up and I have to lower my expectations too, even though it is very difficult for me too. But I am grateful for every day that we can be together and he helps me in every way. He was sick for about 14 days but now he is better again and is making sick visits again in town. He has been nominated as doctor for a large old-people's home being set up nearby under Sister Oberin, but we hope that it will take a while.

Incidentally, this home will bring people from the two urban homes where I worked. The home where Ottole was is also being moved.

So enough about our life and experiences here, now I'm going to answer your nice letters. Is Max with you again? And who will be with you on your wedding anniversary? My thoughts for sure and also my most heartfelt wishes that you will never have to be apart on any other anniversary! Is Uncle M. sending you money for you to live off? I will soon write to dear Friedel who wrote me such a lovely letter again – that will be my next longer letter. I am so happy that they have such good news of their children, Miriam and Walter; it's good that both of them are developing so well and are staying with such good people. The fact that Ottole has gone to other people really hurts me in one way because his foster parents were especially nice and fine and good people. But I think they would not have given the little child away unless they really had to; probably it wasn't possible financially any longer. And then I think that they would only have put the child in a really reliable family where he would be looked after just as well. What such a little being has already had to go through – so much change! But I hope it won't damage him and if he's anything like his mother he will find interest and joy in everything new. Such a shame that Margot so rarely sent me letters from Mrs Ware. (It seems that 'Margot' was the conduit for relaying information from the Ware's and she probably withheld the news that I had been transferred to an orphanage. I have no idea who she was.) *That was really remiss of her since she was in such close contact with her. Are you still in contact with Margot? I asked Manner to get hold of letters. I would really like to know more about Ottole's new living arrangements. Maybe Dorale* (Dora the sister of Flora who had long lived in London) *will write.*

You will also have received news from the loved ones. I am in constant contact and as much as I can I'm sending them necessities. The Adolfs always write especially lovingly and gratefully; they send heartfelt greeting to you through me and they told me to let you know that they will do everything they possibly can to look after Gromele and Emma. I will do this too. Aunty is doing better but she's really suffering from the cold since there's hardly any heating and she's always anxious and worrying……. Gromele is doing well. She had a terrible cold with a cough and bronchitis but Aunty is really looking after her wonderfully. The Foedchens wrote really happily a few days ago – the new aunt is apparently really a wonderfully nice person. Aunt Emma writes very enthusiastically about her. They wrote such a loving and grateful letter because I sent them a big parcel with all sort of useful things for their wedding.

I'm in contact a lot with the dear W's. Just imagine mother, Mrs W is having another child; it should have come around the 26th Feb but she wrote today that she is still waiting. It's a breech birth and last time (7 years ago) she had a caesarean for this reason. She is very worried – I hope everything goes well. Trudel is doing an apprenticeship in a bookshop, Hansel is at school, and he is still in the same place as always. Nobody knows what will happen with him when the home closes and he is moved. You were asking about Rosa Gellhorn. But I've heard nothing at all from her. It's my fault of course since I haven't written, but I just don't get the chance. In the meantime it's now the 3rd March and today is Purim (a

Jewish Festival). *Yesterday evening we celebrated and had coffee and cakes (a big, fat piece for everyone together with cheese – I baked the cake on Sunday morning). Today we didn't have the soup like you used to make, Mum, but we had mushroom soup, roast gammon and potato salad. "Our daily bread..." father, I wish that for you every day. At the moment I have to cook everything myself because Mrs Becker, who always helps me so much, is ill. But I really enjoy it and I'm happy that I've got such a routine going. The residents are always content and they are doing well.*

So now the page is full and I'm going to stop so that I can finally get the letter sent off....So I wish that things will change for the better soon and I send all of you the warmest greeting and many kisses,

Your Tea

PS The XXX's sent a bottle of wine which I'll send on to Gromele

Thea was writing very regularly at this difficult time. She again typed a long letter to the family via Manne and his new wife Louisa on 19th March 1942:

My dear Mannlein and Louisa, Alfred and Lorle,

Today is Sunday and as I was planning to write to you along came your letter that Mannlein sent on the 14.4. Thank you from the bottom of my heart for your lovely detailed report. I can believe that it is often bitterly hard for you to live in these circumstances, separated and often lonely, lacking many things and worrying about each other and your loved ones. But there is only one thing we can do: keep on going, clench your teeth and keep on going. I also resolve to do this every day and ask God for the strength to do it. Thank you, dear Alfred, for your advice not to overreach myself; you are right and I have also promised my dear, loyal friend to think about myself and to watch my health, now he can't do it for me. But it is hard to cope with such a loss.

The last few days were just so awful. When the terrible news came at the end of March that he would be one of the ones who had to leave us (to go to a concentration camp)*, I knew what would happen. He was supposed to have gone along as* *the medical transport director but he was too ill to take on this job. Even without this work, it would have been impossible for him to have borne the stress and exhaustion. We both knew that. You can only be released if you are absolutely incapable of travelling: he was examined by a doctor but he learned that he would in any case have to go with them to the collection camp in Stuttgart. There was no other solution but this unspeakably tragic one. Two weeks ago today – on Easter Sunday – he closed his eyes for ever. It seems to me like an eternity – a long, scary eternity. Maybe God will bring us all together again and then I'll be able to tell you what kind of a man he was. He was indeed a wonderful person, an incredibly hard-working doctor, and he meant everything to me – everything. Through him, I've experienced many good and wonderful things; he enriched and deepened my life in every way, as doctor, as a person, as friend and mentor. He loved and adored me so much and it's a small comfort to me that I could bring him happiness and joy in his last few months. He had already considered his life to be over but he came to life again, became young and cheerful and loved life again. But everything is gone now and I have to get to the point where I can be glad that he now has the peace that he so longed for. There are times when I tell myself how good it is that he overcame everything.*

And now my work has to help me – it is a comfort for me. You will have seen from my note to Manne that both of my assistants had to leave me. Mrs Krips, the older one, has been really helpful in these difficult weeks – she went through everything with us and has often been a comfort and strength for me. She is a mature and rational person, clever and talented, and was a great worker: we will really miss her because she worked with all her heart and soul. She took over when I was on holiday, someone I really could trust. My girl, Ida, was a real doer but terribly stupid and sloppy. I had a lot of trouble with her but I'm still sorry to see her go. In their place I now have Paula Adelsheimer. She isn't very experienced at housework and is more of a nurse. But she is learning her way around and I hope we'll manage the work together. The inmates have to help out more, but it's hard to rely on such old and needy people. I will get some help every now and then for the washing and ironing and so on. A really nice inmate has largely taken over the cooking – she does it as well or better than me. I'm not scared of the work – I can do it really easily and I promise you that I am looking after myself as much as I can.

The weather is so nice again here and it would have been so good if Dr Ess. could have recuperated in the garden. Everything is late this year. Winter was really hard and long, but now everything is growing crazily – you can see it happening. We had almost two weeks of good weather and nature is looking better if not life for us. This terrible war – what is going to happen? – Heilbronn will soon be empty of us. The only survivor is Mr Igersheim and his sister. Elderly people like the Rosenthals (who are older than 67) were sent to Haigersloch where the Spiers were (they were in a convalescent home) – they are doing OK there but it's pretty isolated. Lots of people from there go to Stuttgart where Lotte was. Up to 65 are going there next week [this was the collecting point for transport to a concentration camp]. *I can rarely go to town since I would have to walk there from the station.*

Maybe I'll be able to get permission to drive – but that's not clear yet.

I'm in constant contact with all our loved ones. Gromele is doing relatively well, Aunt Emma is really trying hard but it's difficult to get anything: I send things whenever I can. The tumour is growing but it doesn't cause her any pain, it just weakens her. I would so like to visit Gromele, but it's impossible. The Adolfs write so nicely and are really thoughtful about my suffering. We would be so glad to see each other again. The Ismars (Flora's brother) *sent some wonderful tea, so nice of them – definitely not a small sacrifice. They are doing better now. Uncle is working in the community and they got news from Mannlein and were happy about that. I got a confirmation from the Persikaners that they received the money. They are not allowed to write. I have heard nothing from Lotte but we hear that people in this place are doing OK and have somewhere decent to stay. Lotte's mother complains that she is living terribly and all the excitement made her ill. Maybe I can help.*

… Thea then details all the people around who have been transported or died ..

So my loves, I plan to write soon even if only a postcard a week, just to ensure you don't worry and keep up with things. You really don't need to worry about me. I am forcing myself to be reasonable – to go to bed early and eat well and I also have nice acquaintances in Heilbronn who I spend my afternoons with. We were often together the four of us – the doctor and me. A young mixed couple. Fritz Landauer was the owner of Landauer Machol. They live very nicely and take good care of me. They valued Dr E a lot too. Alfred – can you remember him? When you visited us in the Asyl, he drank coffee with us – do you remember? Now I really wish you get to the nice place again where you already spent a few months and felt at home and that you don't have financial concerns and that you are soon together again. More than anything I urge you to keep resolutely on and hold your head high.

Your Tea.

She relates how with the help of one of her old residents, a horticulturalist, the garden is producing salads and fruit in relative abundance, despite all the grim events around. Clearly, The loss of Dr Essinger was a massive blow. No doubt, in other times and circumstances they would have married ....

Then on 21st March 1942 'Dear Uncle Ludwig (This is Dr Schmal), Thanks for your kind letter. I've written to my brother again to inform him. I just want to tell you that I'm just as well as ever. I'm working and healthy. It's very warm here and the snowdrops are in blossom in the garden. It's good that the terrible winter is over. We won't be able to get Matzos (Jewish unleavened bread) this year, though we have a few left over from last year, hopefully enough for this evenings Passover festival...... We just had an anniversary remembrance of beloved Julius, my husband. He is at peace.'

On the 7th April of the same year she wrote to Manne 'I've been wanting to write to you and our dear parents for a while but have just had the most awful experience. Dr Essinger, my kind, loyal, best friend is dead! Last night, the 5th, he closed his eyes for ever. He was supposed to go the same *route as Lotte and the Persikaners [other family members – referring to their transport to a concentration camp] but he couldn't do it, it is so sad. Four people were to be transported from our small home: one crippled patient, my two girls and the doctor. I have a replacement for the girls but she is an inexperienced worker. We'll have to see how it works out. Today is the funeral. The transport is supposed to be between the 10th and 15th. I want to be strong and courageous and forget myself in my work. A letter came from our parents via Schmal, through Mrs Fritz, who has also now been transported.'*

Dr Essinger committed suicide with a pill overdose, rather than go to a concentration camp. He had been a significant doctor in Heilbronn for years, much loved by all particularly during the depression when he treated the poor without cost. As with all Jewish doctors, the Nazis revoked his licence and he scraped a living for years until he found his role in the Picard house. Today, there is a street in Heilbron named after him.

Manne was able to reply and on the 17th she wrote *'You received my sad postcard and I your happy one – thanks. I want to let you know that you don't need to worry about me. It is just so terribly lonely and sad. I have to get used to this destroyed life and that is not easy. There is nothing that Dr Essinger and I did not share – joy, pain - and I could go to him with every need. We spent every free moment together, I accompanied him on his sick rounds and he helped me with a lot of my work – nothing was too small for him. There is only one good thing to come out of this; he is now in peace. He didn't have to experience all the terrible things that await others. It will be so much lonelier here after the time of mourning. Work is my only comfort.'*

Then on 24th April she again wrote to Manne, now the hub of the family: *'All week I have been wanting to send you a birthday letter for the 24th but never got round to it because we are so terribly busy. It is as Alfred says – work is my only succour. Dear Manne, I miss home so much and I can only forget myself in my work. It is now six weeks since Dr Essinger died, what a sad time. I received lovely letters from my parents and Friedel. As soon as I can I'll write back. Sometimes I'm OK and eat and sleep fine. Well, I'll write more soon. I've heard nothing about little Otto for some time, which is also hard for me.'*

Her last letter to Manne before being transported to Theresianstadt was on 14th August 1942. *'Say goodbye .... We're travelling in the middle of next week. Of course, I now have an unbelievable amount of work with the travel date being so close. Since all 22 patients are to go it is easier, especially for me. I think we'll cope with it alright and I'm actually quite confident. I can handle most things and think it will go OK. There's no reason to be scared. Incidentally, we are not travelling alone but will be part of a big group. Lotte's mother and aunt for example.'*

Amazingly, a year later on 22nd September 1943 she wrote a postcard to Manne again. *'My dear loved ones, I would be so happy if you could let me know of any news of little Otto, my son. I hope there is no reason for me to be concerned about you as you need to be concerned about me. I have been doing very well the whole of my time here. I'm working as a nurse and find lots of joy in my work, am healthy and feel young and full of beans! So write soon; the post works well here; letters, parcels and packages arrive regularly and are delivered promptly. Greetings from Aunt Emma and Feodor* (her father's brother).'

I am certain that this last letter was written under duress. It is totally different in its writing and its style, as well as being quite unbelievable. At this time the SS were working hard to sanitise and beautify the Theresianstadt ghetto, prior to a visit from the Red Cross. They forced inmates to write glowing letters concerning their treatment. The SS spent months 'improving' the appearance of the camp, starting by sending batches of 5000 to Auschwitz where they were gassed, to minimize the apparent overcrowding. They planted gardens and introduced a bandstand into the town centre, introduced park benches, and built cafes in the park, previously out-of-bounds for inmates. Everywhere was tidied up and a kindergarten was started as well as concerts in which the Jewish musicians played. They succeeded in fooling the Red Cross totally. Theresianstadt was a garrison town built by the Austrian emperor in 1840, in what is now the Czech Republic. Being walled it proved ideal to convert into a concentration camp. It was the most cynical act of the Nazi regime who tried to present it as a benevolent act towards Jews.

A year later on 19th October 1944 she was transferred to Auschwitz and probably gassed on arrival together with thousands of others.

A footnote regarding the thoroughness of the SS in tracing and recording all Jews who left the country is of interest. They seemed to be fascinated with me, no doubt intending my extermination on taking over Great Britain. Recording me with 'Israel' added as a middle name (as with all male Jews; females had Sara added similarly) they tracked my movements in a 5-page dossier.

Chapter 3

Nearly Christian

In their final note to the National Childrens' Home, the Ware's suggested that I was beginning to show jealousy of their own children and as a consequence showed some 'messy' behaviour around the house. Hence their further suggestion that I might benefit from living with similarly situated children 'and once removed to the impersonal atmosphere of an Institution .... I would immediately develop into a normal healthy boy'. I must say that puts a much greater philosophical understanding on a 6 year old than seems likely. I fear that dear Harry just needed to have fewer responsibilities given his precarious existence. Whatever the case, the Princess Alice Orphanage was definitely a bit wary of taking in a 'disturbed' refugee child and only agreed as a temporary measure and after an assurance from a child psychologist that I was perfectly normal. I can quite imagine the discussions taking place there of this disturbed, illegitimate, German refugee and orphan, with no birth certificate, possibly half Jewish and brought up as a strict vegetarian and Nature Cure child. How on earth do we feed, care and deal with his foibles?

Whatever the case, I arrived in Birmingham on Monday 10th November 1941, escorted by Mr George Lee of the Christian Council for Refugees from Germany and Central Europe, my costs being 10/- per week to be paid by the Riversmead Fund.

It seems that all the hoo-ha about my dubious condition was a storm in a teacup. I do recall my arrival at Wand House for boys at the Orphanage. I remember being puzzled by the long, rough wood tables and chairs. I was presented with a plate of food consisting of 'batter pudding', took one bite and was heaving at the appalling taste. I refused to eat any more and was told that I would not get anything else until I had eaten that. I was quite happy with that solution and eventually I did get something else (to this day I still can't enjoy e.g. Toad-in-the-hole or Yorkshire pudding from that experience!). I must have sounded rather posh to the other kids as I was ribbed for not wanting the salt passed on to me with 'No thanks, I don't like salt; it's bitter'. I was enrolled at New Oscott Infants School and the following May received a report indicating that I was *'very popular with the school teacher'* my conduct was good and in general *'A bright, intelligent child'*.

In the interim I had had my tonsils out and got used to a completely new diet, with often mouldy, white, 2lb loaves of bread, some meat, boiled-to-death cabbage and rarely much in the way of potatoes or fruit. I could never get used to fish and refused it with the same battle as before. To me it tasted like the smell of the laundry, where I had been befriended by one of the ladies working there and whom I often visited.

The Orphanage was run by 'Sisters' and was almost self-contained in that it had its own hospital, laundry, large grounds where older children were taught growing vegetables and some farming and even their own church, where we attended each Sunday. I seemed to get on with the staff, especially Sister Jean Phipps and Sister Maud, while the Head, Mr Roycroft, was relieved to find me relatively normal. Indeed, as times went by he became positively effusive. I distinctly recall missing the loving touch that I must have experienced from Armyne and my mother beforehand. On one occasion we visited some nearby woodland on a slope down to a river. I think it must have rung a bell in my memory of Edinburgh and The Cotswolds perhaps as I really enjoyed the trip. So much so that I remember rolling down a slope and inadvertently knocking myself out on a tree that got in the way. I recall waking up on the lap of Sister Jean, who was stroking my head and looking concerned. I relished the comforting moment as much as the rest of the day out.

'This boy has made splendid progress, both at school (now Green Lane Junior School) *where the teachers are delighted with him, and in the House. His incontinence has completely disappeared .....'* my report after one year recorded. I remember often being in the Air Raid shelter overnight and hating the sound of the siren – especially the All Clear, oddly. But I also recall the delight us boys had next morning looking for pieces of shrapnel – prized possessions – or bomb craters. Our route to school down Chester Road seemed to be the way to some prisoner-of-war camps and the buses filled with grim-faced Germans that passed us were greeted with 'Heil Hitler' signs from us with

a finger under our noses for a moustache, while the happy smiling Italians were greeted with waves. Rarely, we met American soldiers and learnt quickly to say 'got any gum chum?' which always worked – a real treat.

Presents at Christmas were a rarity and birthdays none existent. In my first year there I received a teddy bear, though I had no idea where it came from. Armyne maybe? However, not long after I caught chicken pox and was in the hospital for a short spell. On leaving my teddy was, sadly, incinerated. I really missed that bear.

The next few half-yearly Orphanage reports continued in the same vein as the earlier ones until July 1944 when storm clouds began to build on my horizon. Letters from The Refugee Children's Movement Limited were sent to Mr Roycroft concerned that I was being brought up as a Christian. Mr J.A.B. Gale, a member of that committee noted that *'The Riversmead Committee has asked for a report on his progress and his religious upbringing and I should be glad to have a note from you about these matters. I do not think any action is likely but the RCM is never tired of stirring up some sort of trouble of this kind.'*

The report was duly sent reporting that *'this lad is getting on splendidly. He is bright and intelligent and doing well at school and is a thoroughly good youngster. He is not the slightest bit like the report we received of him before he came into the home. Otto attends our Morning Prayers AND Sunday Services. I cannot bring him up as a practising Jew and the reason is obvious.'*

The RCM continued to press poor old Mr Roycroft to arrange for appropriate religious education, with Rev Simpson discussing with Rev Litten, who was the nearest member of the Jewish community to handle this and asking for me to be exempt from prayers and instruction. I can imagine these bumbling vicars with no experience of running a Christian orphanage, chatting over afternoon tea in their gaiters, determining the unhappy future of a refugee orphan.

Mr Roycroft dug his heels in, declaring the total impractibility of their suggestions and that he considered it was seriously inadvisable to move Otto just now.

Several letters later the RCM officer, a Mr Van der Zyl, reported that *'we are still having difficulty with the Jewish community over this boy's religious upbringing. .... the best course is for a representative of the Jewish community to have an interview with you to see if an amicable arrangement can be made. If such an arrangement cannot be made, Otto will have to leave.'*

On 9th November, after several more letters and a visit from two Jewish folk, it was concluded that in no way could the orphanage make a special case of one child without making him a 'peculiar' person, as they phrased it. It was reluctantly proposed by Mr Roycroft that *'he be transferred to a small Jewish hostel in Manchester where there were about 20 boys in a similar situation to Otto. It was not run on strictly orthodox lines and thus the break might not be too severe.'*

Several more letters and forms were passed between the various organisations involved and finally on the 18th January 1945 permission was granted for my transfer to the Jewish Refugees

Hostel, 9 [later the house number was changed to 401] Wilmslow Road, Withington, Manchester.

Mr Roycroft was evidently distraught at the new upheaval in the life of a boy well settled into orphanage life and doing well in school as well as in Wand House. He escorted me, just short of 10 years old, to the Hostel on Thursday, 2nd February 1945. I remember the day well. A strange man, with frizzy hair, cold eyes – even when he smiled – and an odd accent was introduced to me as the warden, Mr Siegfried Alexander. I also met a sad-looking woman, Mrs Strauss, the cook, again with a rather cold demeanour. This was a poor start for a bewildered child and I watched Mr Roycroft leave with trepidation. This stay was to be for 7 years, after only 3 years in Birmingham.

Chapter 4

Nearly Jewish – again

The hostel was a large, imposing, detached building set in unfussy grounds, with a large drive and, one bright feature – a conker tree – in the front garden. A path to the right led through to the rear which had a cobbled yard and an unkempt piece of grassland bordered by trees that looked good for climbing. Up several steps, the front porch led into a wide, high-ceilinged, lino-clad hallway with imposing pillars either side, with a large lounge on the left and even larger dining room on the right. Further to the right was Mr Alexander's room, one I rarely even saw into and never entered. On the left was the kitchen, still with its old fashioned kitchen range and fireplace, and a large pantry, cooking and sink area. From the kitchen, stairs led down into the cellar, half of the rooms of which were locked with, I always presumed, the previous occupants belongings. We used to peep through the keyhole to try to discover its contents. A coal cellar with a shoot from the cobbled back yard and a coal-fired central heating boiler occupied another two rooms and a workshop with a high, hatch window to the outside left of the house. The furthest and darkest room was used only for shoe cleaning.

Opposite the dining room a wide staircase with a magnificent shiny wooden balustrade, which took my fancy for sliding down, led to 5 bedrooms, one occupied by Mrs Strauss. Again, I never saw the inside of that room. Further stairs led to what must have been servants quarters, kept in readiness in case of more inmates arriving suddenly. One bath and sink sufficed for us all and a rota for a weekly bath was in place. Two of the 'titches' as we were known, bathed together. Each bedroom had several beds, each with a locker. Having no possessions meant I was given a bed with the minutest of lockers. I was quickly informed of the work system that operated every Sunday.

All the schoolboys were each allocated a job on a rotation basis. These comprised sweeping and polishing the lino floors – the hall was one job and dining room + lounge another – boot and shoe cleaning for the whole house, washing/drying up for the week, etc. We were expected to keep our beds made and rooms tidy and darn our socks and any other holed garment, which were mostly hand-me-downs. I enjoyed the Hall polishing and after applying the polish would tie rags to my feet and skate up and down the long hall until it shone like glass. Polishing the shoes and boots in the dark and dank cellar was a real pain.

The inmates were a strange bunch with the oddest of names. Of my own age was Maurice Freifeld and Peter Dannenberg (known as 'nipper' he being the youngest – and thickest); then there was Herbert Rindl and Feodor Scheinmann, both academically bright and interested in science; Pieche, Bodo, brothers Hans and Oscar, and Schloime, the son of Frau Strauss, Gerd, Heinz and others were all working in engineering workshops or gardening. Kurt Bernheim, known to us as Jelly, was still at school and was a passionate reader. Peter Katzer was to become my friend and protector, being as strong as a horse. Schloime was a tall, foul-mouthed, chain-smoking bully and would make us nippers his slaves when he could. Another interesting character turned out to be a room-mate, Jacky Batton. Despite being disabled from birth, having a clubbed foot, maimed arm and enlarged head, he was a thoughtful and pleasant chap and was the waker-upper for the hostel. He also was a keen, if slow, hiker. He worked at Bradshaw's Guides as a proof reader. To me this was the ultimate awful job but he loved it and knew everything there was to know about train timetables. Lots of strange accents and bouts of German were spoken. New residents came and others left, often to go to USA to family who had emigrated there, after the war finished a few months later.

Bernard Reil was 16 when he arrived from Czechoslovakia speaking not a word of English. Within 6 months he had passed his School Certificate examinations and took up full-time education in the Royal Technical College, Salford, studying Mechanical Engineering. Norbert Topper did something similar and was an early leaver for USA. Some, like Gerd Goldman had seen military service and he obviously suffered mentally from the experience, unlike cheerful and chubby Bodo. Heinz had also returned from army duty. He had his name changed – not to John Smith but, much to my surprise – to Harry Jacobi! He entered the Jewish ministry later.

91

Willy Flehner arrived in his early 20s, a refugee who had spent much of the war avoiding the Nazis in his home country of Norway. Near the war end he had managed to escape to England, unlike his parents who disappeared as so many other Jews did. He became a journalist and wrote of his experiences in a book, though I cannot remember if it was ever published. I recall reading chunks of the manuscript.

The Jewish aspect of the hostel was very low key. For a little while a rabbi came weekly to give me Hebrew lessons but soon gave me up as a hopeless case. We were allowed to go to synagogue on Saturdays but very few availed themselves of the chance. Since neither 'The Old Man' (Mr Alexander) or Frau Strauss went, we got the message. However, there was a small incentive to go. We were given the bus fare to travel to the centre of Manchester then on to the synagogue in Cheetham Hill and after the service there was an excellent buffet. Peter and I sometimes went – occasionally playing truant from synagogue and wandering around Manchester centre instead. We were caught out once when a hostel official espied us and we were given a hard time. As with Christmas and Easter, the hostel kept up the Passover ritual at Easter time and Chanukah at Christmas. Since Passover involved another fine meal we all enjoyed it even if the Hebrew recitations were as meaningful as Chinese to me.

The Old Man was a brooding and frustrated chap. He had an estranged wife who occasionally appeared, a frightening witch-like woman who nevertheless tried to mother us squirming titches. He was, apparently, an accomplished artist and had been an actor in Berlin before the war. Now he was a silent, Manchester Guardian-reading intellectual, feared by the titches. He had a tendency to suddenly loose his cool and fly into an impressive temper. In the dining room we had a gas fire and were allowed to make toast at breakfast time, using toasting forks. Maurice had spread his toast with jam and was eating it with relish, spreading the jam round his face. Suddenly Vesuvius erupted and the Old Man rushed up behind Maurice and belted him around the ear. Maurice had raised his hands to protect his head, still holding the toast. The jammy mess hurtled into the wall and slid down impressively and we all had to work hard to stifle giggles. The Old Man stalked out with his paper and the room collapsed in laughter, even tearful Maurice joining in. I had many such events with Mr Alexander.

The food was really very good; Mrs Strauss, who clearly detested the Old Man, was a fine cook and even convinced me to try the cod, explaining that it was 'royal cod' exactly like the king ate. She also made a fine job of cabbage, cooking it in so many different ways. We received 1d per week pocket money and also had our sweet rations. I would swap some of my ration for a spell on a neighbour's bike or sell them at school. I also made a little extra money selling conkers in the season; we had a rota of boys protecting our tree from invaders and had many a scrap in doing so. In this way, Peter and I would go to Platt Fields Park and spend our saved up money on tea and buns in the café there, feeling like a pair of toffs. It left nothing for boating on the lake.

A few months after my arrival, VE Day – Victory in Europe - was announced on Friday 8th May, with banner headlines in the Old Man's Manchester Guardian, which he passed round for us all to read. The worst of the war was over; Hitler was dead and his henchmen imprisoned awaiting trial. The hostel celebrated and I was sent into Withington to buy cigarettes! Not that I smoked but most of the working boys did as well as the Old Man. We put on a show with Mr Alexander excelling, using his old stage experience by writing humorous sketches. We had an ancient gramophone with a few scratchy records, from which I learnt all the songs. I and Schloime were partnered doing a Bing Crosby-Johnny Mercer style number that went to their tune on one of those records; I was Mr Titch and he was Mr Working Boy. 'Oh Mr Working Boy, Oh Mr Working Boy' 'What is on your mind this evening Mr Titch?' 'Everybody's making fun, of the way our hostel's run, is it possible that there's a major hitch?' ...... and several more such verses. It went down a treat. Not far away was a similar girls hostel and they were all invited. We were invited back to repeat the event with an even bigger audience. I noticed later that Sonia was in a quiet corner kissing Bernard ....

Soon after the end of the war I received a document sent out by some authority in

Czechoslovakia. It was half a page long and was clearly one of several carbon copies so not easily legible. It informed me of my mother's fate, being gassed on arrival at Auschwitz, just months before the war end. It left me a bit dazed, not due to the pain of loss so much as the fact that I couldn't remember anything about her. I had no memory of or rapport with that loving soul that had brought me into the world and loved and cared for me for over 4 years. I felt bad that I did not feel the remorse that I should have felt.

Being 10 years old, I was not far off the 11-plus examination and was enrolled at nearby Old Moat School, a tough and unpleasant place with bullying the norm – especially if you happened to be called Otto, a damned German. My form mistress was another vicious, witch-like spinster who disliked children in general. She wielded a large wooden ruler which she used regularly for punishment. On one occasion she wacked a girl across her hand; the girl burst into tears saying 'I'm going home to tell my Dad so put that in your pipe and smoke it!' The whole class collapsed in laughter. However, she didn't improve my chances of passing exams.

Surprisingly, there was no pressure from the hostel to perform at school. The most encouragement came from other older inmates. One such was a recent arrival from Yugoslavia, Ivan Danicic, with an impressively strong accent and a brilliant knowledge of maths and sciences. He took it upon himself to teach maths to Nipper. After an hour of getting nowhere, he suddenly exploded with 'Neepa, you EEeeediot!!' and gave up the task. Petro was also brilliant at ball games. Once we were in the lounge when a mouse appeared. He tossed a metal ashtray at the mouse and caught it with its tail stuck out of a slot.

Encouraged by Jelly, I had joined the nearby library and regularly borrowed non-fiction books about science and discoveries. Very much to my surprise, the hostel was given a subscription to a number of magazines. These included 'The Illustrated London News' – brilliant pictures and news items, 'Picture Post' a similar type of magazine, 'Nature' – now regarded as the premiere science research publication in the world and others. I was an unlikely but regular browser. I particularly enjoyed tackling the crossword puzzles in Picture Post. Listening to the radio was ever popular but I rarely heard pop songs. If Beethoven, Mozart or music by other famous classical composers was played we titches were warned to keep quiet. I probably know all the pieces by the first two composers from the drilling I endured. I also especially enjoyed Churchill's speeches, Letter from America and the Radio Doctor. Also, games like chess, draughts and card games like Solo, as well as Monoply were regularly indulged in as were jigsaw puzzles. Us titches also played out a lot, a favourite game being 'whip tin' where the person who is 'on' has to count to 10 with his eyes shut while another person kicks the tin as hard as he could. He had to retrieve the tin and put it in its place then find the hiding kids, hitting the tin before they did. The best hiding places were in the cellar where exit via the high workshop window was worth the pain and allowed a circumnavigation of the hostel. Cricket in the back yard was impressive since the cobbles allowed some most unexpected 'spin' bowling. But of all the activities, cycling was my favourite escape.

On one summer occasion I 'rented' neighbour Frank's bike with some sweet coupons and cycled to the canal at Marple, a good few miles south of Withington. Arriving there I swam in the canal, dried myself on my vest and cycled back, exhilarated. On arrival back home I was met on the stairs going up to my room by a furious Old Man. I had clean forgotten that a lady inspector was coming that day to speak to the kids individually. He grabbed me by the neck and shook me like a rag doll, and threw me down the stairs. I was, of course, crying and bruised by this time. He commanded 'wipe your eyes and go into that room', which I did. There was a kindly soul who straight away asked me my name and then 'How do you like it here in the hostel?' Obviously I said 'Oh, it's fine', not daring to say otherwise. I fully understand the silence of abused kids, though there was never anything other than brutality, arising from the Old Man's temper.

I half-passed my 11-plus examination it seems. I was to go to Didsbury Central School for Boys, an innovative type of school where in the third year pupils could specialise in either Commercial subjects – shorthand and book-keeping, or Woodwork and Metalwork. What an odd choice! I really didn't fancy either, being more interested in science, but that was not an option. The first day was Rag Day when the new intake were given a rough, very rough - introduction to the school, with the all-male staff turning a blind eye. Our class included Atkins, my chief rival in Maths. I used to enjoy being faster than him at solving Algebra equations. Fatty Brown, a pleasant lad who did well academically but was, like me, a non-sportsman. Tagger was the rough and tough little blighter who made my life a misery with his bullying and slurs as to my presumed Nazi sympathies. Franky Jones was an early sexual developer who kept us posted on what we should know about girls. Bretty and Ellwood were two nerds who knew lots of interesting things about science. Plenty of other various good and bad lads made up the class. In the form above ours was one of the dreaded Wilson's, the local hoodlum family with a drunken, wife-beating man at the head. His older brother with his henchmen would try to steal our dinner money at break times to buy fags and we all kept well clear of that bunch.

My curriculum included English Literature and Language, Maths, Physics, History, Geography, RI (not Jewish, but Christian), French, Art and PE. No chemistry or biology was available. Being poor at Woodwork I ended up opting for Commercial subjects as it was taken by our popular form master, Mr Morter. While I hated the book-keeping bit, I thoroughly enjoyed Pitman's shorthand. The English teacher, Mr Roberts, who like most of the teachers had just come out of the army, took an instant dislike to me, which proved unfortunate for me. He had a sergeant major's stance and moustache and a habit of emitting a fine spray of spit as he talked. The spray seemed to be aimed at me mostly. I can only think it was the 'Otto factor' again. I tried my darnedest to get more than 6/10 for an essay but without success, my endeavours always being covered in red ink. On one occasion I had to write an essay on 'A woodland glade'. Having just finished reading 'The White Company' by Sir Arthur Conan Doyle (incidentally a friend of Sir Fabian Ware from my Cotswold days), I started my essay, copied a big chunk of Sir Arthur, then finished it off myself. Poor old Doyle; his work received even more red ink than I did and we managed 5/10! That convinced me to stop trying – and I eventually had to re-sit my English Language exam, by then with a new teacher. I was always up at the top end in Maths and Physics, enjoyed and did well in History, with another good teacher, Mr Dalkin, and Geography with Mr Luckman – Lucy to us – who carried a 'wand of magic wisdom' around the class but was nevertheless a kindly man. Our French master had been in the Foreign Legion and it was really easy to get him off the subject of the lesson to tell us tales from his Legion days. Woodwork and metalwork were taken by a lovely old chap, Mr Huddleston, who was very forgiving of my impressive lack of talent. He used to go round singing 'on the waste wood side of the line' but I still botched up my mortise and tenon joints. I once set out to make an octagonal egg stand for four eggs with a carrying handle at the centre. Trying to even up the chamfered edges, I eventually end up with a teapot stand instead. It was good fun but I was pretty useless at it.

These were the days of pea-soup fogs in autumn and winter, when most household heating was by coal and before the Clean Air Act was declared. Manchester was a highly industrialised city and high up the pea-soup league. Our hostel was on the main commuter route south from central

Manchester, Wilmslow Road being an extension of Oxford Road a main thoroughfare in the city. On such dark and impenetrable evenings, us titches would take turns to stand at our front gate with a scarf around our mouths and noses, informing lost souls where they were – and earning the odd penny, threepenny bit or sometimes even a tanner. Our faces would become quite smudged with the dirty air. Across the road was a church with an impressively tall and thin steeple which was a useful landmark for travellers, though invisible, as was anything more than a yard away. I note that the church has completely disappeared today, being replaced by apartments though the hostel building is still there.

Sadly, I never excelled at sports or athletics, which were considered the ultimate sign of a good student. I loved cricket but was always placed in the outfield and batted well down the order, while my bowling was too erratic to be useful. The problem lay with the fact that my left-handedness was ignored by the sports master. He insisted that I bat and bowl right-handed. A group of us who were similarly poor at sports found a joint interest in science and started a 'Mystery & Science Club'. Today I suppose we would be the nerds of our class. Our first venture was to make Crystal sets, which proved amazingly easy, cheap and effective. I managed to buy bits from an Army & Navy store including a tatty pair of earphones and rigged up a fantastic aerial from my bedroom to the Conker tree. The strongest signal I managed to pick up was Radio Moscow English Service, which I listened to under my bedclothes at night, but the making and improving of the set was the real interest. From there we next made one-valve sets and learnt Morse code, communicating on the shortwave 40 metre band. We also did crazy chemistry experiments, melted down lead soldiers and made moulds of our own and even dabbled with séances, frightening the life out of ourselves by one or other giving the table a violent tilt. Through this group I became good friends with Brian Ellwood, chief nerd, and was always welcome at his house. His father was a senior policeman and on one occasion in 1946 he managed to get us into Maine Road, the football ground of Manchester City. That Saturday, Manchester United played against Arsenal, since

United's ground, Old Trafford, had been bombed in the war. With a crowd of 82,000, all standing, us kids were handed down to sit on the touchline. I watched in awe as United won 5-2.

Herbert Rindl finished at grammar school and found a job at The Shirley Institute in the textile business. Feo left school and enrolled for an external London University degree course in Chemistry at The Royal Technical College, Salford . I was most impressed with his homework exploits and he probably planted a chemistry seed in my brain. Jelly joined a Withington baker near the Scala cinema and I used to enjoy calling in now and again to get a free warm bun. The baker thought the world of Jelly, who was a whirlwind of action in the bakery. They eventually became partners. (Many years later I returned to the bakery to find that Jelly had died not long before). Talking of the cinema, the hostel kids were allowed to go free one evening a week, a real highlight. I saw James Mason, Barbara Stanwick, Jane Russell, Gregory Peck and lots of other famous actors, mostly American, and thoroughly enjoyed the escapism from hostel reality, despite the film's major emphasis on snogging. Ugh! But there was always a cartoon before the main film as well as Pathé Pictorial News.

One day, to my surprise, I received a letter, my first ever. It was from my great aunt Dora, my grandmother's sister, who wrote in a curious, foreign English. I didn't even know I had any family at that stage. She invited me to visit her in London during the summer holidays and also to stay with her nearby sister, Selma. They both lived in Golders Green and sent me the train fare. As I had no memory of my brief earlier stay in London, it sounded an interesting place to visit, though I was unsure about these German-speaking relations. When the day came Jacky Batton urged me to travel from Manchester Central station, via Derbyshire, not the usual Victoria-Exchange direct route. I was captivated by this old-fashioned line through lovely country and always preferred that way until Dr Beeching closed it down. Arriving in London I took the Northern Line tube train – another great experience - to Golders Green and followed my aunt's instructions to find Bridge Lane and her house, number 23, a lovely old rambling property with an untidy garden with fruit trees. She was so delighted to see me and obviously decided that I needed feeding up. Her constant refrain was 'Eat Otto, eat!' and despite her being a vegetarian, she made the most wonderful meals. Her chicken soup, served overflowing in large, Victorian soup plates, was absolutely delicious. She was a spinster, had worked in the Post Office and latterly, before she retired, had been a cook in a wealthy family's household. Despite her advanced years she was great fun and so cheerful, despite her hyper-Germanic twang. Her sister Selma was as opposite as it was possible, a half-empty type with a despairing view of life. (I mentioned in an earlier chapter that her husband had committed suicide due to being badly beaten by Nazi thugs). She had a daughter, Ruth, who was engaged to a very Jewish young chap, Jack, who was always fawning over her and while there I met my mother's older sister, Friedel and her husband Max. They had escaped the war but obviously had suffered much, Max especially, who was now a mentally disturbed old man who did not survive long after my meeting him, another victim of Nazi cruelty. Their daughter Miriam also visited, a vivacious and delightful young woman, engaged to a brash young man, Peter Braun. He was a successful businessman working at the top end of an engineering company while Miriam and Ruth were both typists. I also met Miriam's brother, Walter, a friendly and serious young journalist. Peter and Walter asked me how my Jewish training was going and despaired at my lack of interest. Through this meeting with family I learnt that my grandparents were still alive and now in USA and several other family members were dotted around the world, having escaped or survived the Nazis. No mention was made of my mother. Friedel ended up with my grandparents in Florida, USA while Miriam and Peter settled in Montreal. Walter became editor of The Marathon Echo in upper New York State.

I enjoyed trips to the zoo with Miriam and Peter and on one occasion went to her office and was given a typewriter to have a go at, a novel experience and enjoyable. I would be given a little money to go into London on my own and loved wandering in the then historic – and often bombed out – corners of the centre. The Billingsgate fish market was enthralling. As I wandered down a typical street there, I watched in awe down into cellars where men were rapidly chopping live eels into barrels, all the pieces still squirming and barrels by the score. Rats would rush past me carrying a trophy to some hole. I climbed to the top of the Monument tower, erected to commemorate the Great Fire of London, visited Buckingham Palace, being nearly bowled over by a Grenadier Guardsman as I cornered to the front of the palace. I loved the large parks. On one occasion I went to Hyde Park with Ruth and Jack. They packed me off while they indulged in some serious snogging and were most annoyed when I returned too early.

It was not long after these first family contacts that I was put in touch with local, distant Jewish relatives, George Street and his family and the Kaufmanns. I learnt later that all this family link-up arose from the endeavours of my grandfather. He and his wife, Flora survived Gurs and as soon as they were able emigrated to New York where Flora's brother Fred had lived for years. They were both in their mid-60s and certainly worse for the years of deprivation. Nonetheless, Alfred immediately sought a job as a door-to-door salesman and Flora as a cleaner. In his spare time

Alfred began the process of getting some reparation from the German government for his terrible losses. His tireless endeavours were fruitful in the end and they were able to retire and buy a house in St Petersburg, Florida. He then put his efforts into getting some help for me also. He lived to be 89 and Flora to 94 years.

I must say that I didn't enjoy the many attempts to Judaise me by various surrogates sent by my grandfather. The Street family were, I'm sure, well meaning, but I found their lifestyle foreign and not at all to my taste. He was a business executive for a chemical company, a highly strung man who always seemed about to have a nervous breakdown. His wife was loving but similarly fussy and uptight. The whole German Jewish thing seemed a different world to me and not to my liking. I had learnt to keep my feelings to myself and probably appeared a very shy and withdrawn boy when in this strange cultural environment.

As my 13th birthday loomed I was informed that I had to undergo Bar mitzvah – that is, to become a Jewish man! My grandfather insisted that the hostel arrange this. This isn't an operation – it's a ceremony, which required me to recite reams of Hebrew, read from the Hebrew bible, the Torah, and give a learned discourse on becoming a man. Hmmmm. The only way I could manage this was to learn it all by heart. To me it was a pointless farce but I reluctantly went through with it as young children do. I was the despair of the rabbi who did his best to teach me how to read the weird script, all the etiquette involved in the ceremony, the strange attire needed for the day and so on. Someone had sent me the prayer shawl – a tallit – belonging to Julius, my step-father, encrusted with silver and made of silk. Somehow I bumbled through – then forgot it all and never went back to the synagogue again. The celebration meal was excellent though, as were the first presents I could remember since my teddy bear. They included a Swiss gold watch from my grandparents, a crocodile skin wallet (what do I put in it, I asked Peter) from my unknown and now Swiss uncle Manfred and a Websters Collegiate dictionary from my grandfather (which I still have). My mother's sister Herta in Haifa, Israel sent a crate of Jaffa oranges and continued to send them each year. At last I had something to put in my locker. I discovered I had several other aunts and cousins around the world. Still, the German Jewish aspects were a cultural shock and I was determined not to get too involved.

Grandfather's endeavours were beginning to bear fruit in my cause. One day the Old Man asked me if I would like to buy a brand new bicycle! I wasn't informed as to how much money was available and never was told if there was any more subsequently – and I dare not have asked. However, I was escorted to a bike shop and allowed to choose a shiny electric blue sports bike with 6 gears and dropped handle bars. Wow! I kept it in the cellar and oiled and polished it regularly, never allowing it to look other than new. Now the bus ride to Didsbury on the number 42 followed by the long walk up School Lane, passing the large Capital Cinema was occasionally replaced by a whizzing bike trip and I got to know the country to the south of Manchester quite well.

Around that time, Jacky Batton asked me to join him youth-hostelling on the Yorkshire coast. We walked from Whitby to Scarborough and on to

Robin Hood's Bay in early December in surprisingly mild and dry weather and I really enjoyed this taste of freedom from the hostel.

Reaching the third year a small group of us at school, who had chosen Commercial Subjects, started our studies with Mr Morter, a very patient, cheerful and encouraging man who had spent the war in the navy. Pee, Bee, Tee, Dee, Chay, Jay. The judge said it is paid. Within the first few lessons, writing in pencil, I was surprised how novel Shorthand was and most enjoyed it. We all passed O-level eventually with dictation for 5 minutes at 70 words a minute. Although I passed book-keeping I always have shunned treasurer jobs in any organisation I have since been involved with. Physics, on the other hand was really enjoyable with lots of fascinating demonstrations of magnetism, electricity and motors and boring bits about levers and Mechanical Advantage etc. I remember the master announcing the discovery of the lightest material ever made – expanded polystyrene, and promised to get some to impress us. Another recent invention, the Biro, was, however, not allowed in the school as they were deemed to be bad for handwriting. Pen & ink were far superior, we were told, and most of us still used the old scratchy pens dipped into inkwells in the desk, filled by the ink monitor.

I remember Fatty Brown showing off his Christmas present, a smart, shiny fountain pen that kept writing for ages and I recall being very envious. The large storage room in the hostel cellar was mostly full of junk but I was intrigued by several old kitbags that had been there all my time in the place. One day I decided to have a rummage in one of them. Mostly it was full of rather smelly bits of clothing but one hard item met my fingers, a tube. I pulled it out and to my surprise it was a black German Pelikan fountain pen with a pelican image in white inscribed on the top of the lid. It had a gold clip and gold nib. To my even greater surprise it still wrote – in black. Not the insipid dark brown of our dip pens or the bright blue of Fatty's pen but a deep black like on a five pound note. I could only think that one of the returning soldiers had taken it from some German prisoner-of-war or swapped it for some cigarettes. I showed it around in the hostel and no one made any comments so it became my prized possession and greatly improved my hand-writing. I've used black ink ever since.

The hostel numbers were slowly decreasing as inmates emigrated to USA or left to take up work or further study. Bernard brought home his bride-to-be, a local Manchester girl. New refugees were no longer arriving and it was decided to merge the girl's hostel with the boy's. The girls were much reduced, many getting married, Bodo married Rosie, for example, leaving just a handful of school kids. The girls occupied the attic floor with its own bathroom and Frau Strauss to keep an eye on them. The whole atmosphere of the hostel changed. Even Schloime seemed to moderate his coarse language. I remember also at this time we had a wild character join us, Danny, who had three passions – opera singing as a tenor, wrestling and weight-lifting. He decided to take me in hand and teach me some wrestling and lifting. Down in the cellar I would do push-ups and bench presses but remained as skinny as a lath. However, I really enjoyed wrestling, maybe bringing back the days with Charlie. The next occasion Schloime decided to show off his status to the girls and gave me a push to the floor, I grabbed his ankle, put my foot on his knee and yanked hard. I was gratified when he toppled like a tall pine in a storm. The girls laughed and I was never bullied by him again, though I never gained that Charles Atlas physique and remained a skinbag. Years later a car honked as it passed me on Wilmslow Road; I looked round and it was smiling Danny driving an ancient Rolls with a smart young lady beside him. I never saw him again …… whatever happened to him? I lost contact with most of the boys, though I heard that Schloime died in 2000 aged 73 and Bernard in 2008 aged 76. Willy Flehner is still alive and I'm still in touch with Feo and, recently, Herbert. The Old Man went back to Germany in the late '50s and died there apparently.

I was now receiving several long, complicated forms from a German lawyer working for 'Der Landesamt fur die Wiedergutmachung', apparently an agency for restitution payments to those who suffered loss under the Nazis. They meant nothing to me and I tried hard to ignore them but was bullied by Mr Street and thereby by the Old Man to fill them in and return them.

My final year at school was in turmoil since School Certificate had been supplanted by O Levels which resulted in quite some changes in our teaching. One of the teachers had also been appointed as a careers master and in time I was interviewed – briefly – as to my intentions on leaving school. He suggested I became a reporter which didn't turn me on at all. When asked I said I'd like to become an archaeologist. 'Don't be stupid boy, that's a rich man's hobby'. That was as far as we got. To mention chemistry would have been even dafter but talking one day in a similar vein to Mr Street, who no doubt had been appointed to the same role by my grandfather, I mentioned chemistry. To my surprise he said he would see what he could do for me.

Around this time the headmaster, Mr Kirkpatrick, announced at school assembly that all classes would be suspended for half an hour at 11am and we should all proceed onto the far side of the playing field, near the railway line. No one knew why but at 1110 two curious trains passed down the line, 10,000 and 10,001, the first two diesel locomotives to be introduced onto the British Rail system. We all cheered but I was deeply dissatisfied by their lack of romance; no steam, no whirling rods and pistons, firemen and fires. This, apparently, was progress.

I was coming up to my 16ᵗʰ birthday when I was told that I needed to do something about my nationality. At 16 I would become stateless! As such I would be required to register weekly at the police station. Wow! I did not realise that this was an issue, but applied to become a British citizen smartly. This was granted in July 1951. Just as well as at that time I did not even have a birth certificate, which complicated life somewhat. It would be 50 years before I discovered, through my daughter's efforts, that I did indeed have a Dutch birth certificate. My only proof of existence until that time was my 'Landing Certificate' from my arrival at Harwich in 1939.

To celebrate the completion of O Level examinations, Peter and I decided to visit London on the occasion of the Festival of Britain. This was a centenary re-enactment of the Great Exhibition of 1851 and stalls from all over the world were keen to impress visitors. Grandfather's endeavours had brought a little more restitution money my way and I was fitted for a new suit – a Donegal tweed green – and new shirts, shoes and underclothes, as well as a bit more pocket money. We stayed at Aunt Dora's and travelled in each day to the Festival. What a revelation! I particularly liked the Dome of Discovery, as well as the pretty Nell Gwynn girls with baskets of never-before-seen peaches and other exotic fruits. Britain still had rationing but a certain relaxation was evident at the Festival. Peter had a particular talent for picking up girls and disappeared more than one evening on such assignations.

Returning home to the hostel I discovered that Elly, my nerdy friend had already started work at Factice Research not far from the Hostel, as a lab assistant in a rubber research company. I was envious. However, Mr Street was not idle and came to see me soon after, telling me that a chemical company in Eccles was willing to give me a trial in the research Laboratory. Lankro Chemicals was a company started by a German Jewish refugee, Dr Faulk Heinz Kroch – Dr Krock to the locals – in 1937. Dr Kroch had developed a thriving enterprise in Eccles, being its largest company and a major employer in the town. He was well over 6' tall and built like a bull, with a sabre scar on his cheek from his student days. However, he was the most benevolent and kindly of men, immensely respected and generous to his large workforce. He had a soft spot for employing other refugees and was willing to take on the likes of me despite my total ignorance of chemistry. I didn't even have an interview and was told I had the job of lab. assistant to the Head of Research, Dr Adolf Köbner, another German Jewish refugee who had been a PhD student of the famous Sir Robert Robinson of Oxford University, and joined the company just after the war. Furthermore, the offer was in spite of my not yet having had the results of my O Levels. Mr Street must have sold me a bit too well!

Chapter 5

Nearly a chemist

Fortunately, my O Level results were not too bad and part of the deal at Lankro was that I would enrol at The Royal Technical College, Salford to study one day and evening per week for the National Certificate of Chemistry, a three year course. What a change in one day. In autumn 1951 I rode my bike the 7 miles to Eccles to start at 8am in the lab. I went the longer way via Chorlton cum Hardy despite a bad cobbled bit in order not to be 'bridged' by the Manchester Ship Canal road bridge, which seemed to specialise in opening for canal traffic at rush hour. Arriving nice and early, before any others arrived, I went to Dr Köbner's lab. and sat on a stool, noticing that the electric clock was not working. So I stood on the stool, removed the clock and restarted it, my first bit of research. As I was returning it, in walked a squat, ginger-haired man with a moustache, in blue overalls who said 'What the bloody hell d'you think you're doing?!' I explained and received a long diatribe about putting electricians out of work, Unionism and what I could and could not do. I was truly gobsmacked at my first experience of rampant unionism. He turned out to be the shop steward of the electricians union and, I discovered later, a staunch communist, one of several in the companies blue-collar employees. About that time I had read a smattering about politics and had a vague idealistic respect for Labour policies, protecting the interests of the common worker. I'd also read the Conservative party slogan 'I believe in Private Enterprise' and also seemed to agree with that principle. After my first experience of the Left in action I reckon I shifted markedly towards the right. My views were subsequently reinforced by later experiences.

Slowly people rolled in, Alf Williamson, second in command and a cheerful, chubby character; dapper Edith Hampson, a star research worker; Mrs Herbert, the department secretary, always immaculately turned out; Frank Brimelow, another, more experienced lab. assistant; and finally Dr Köbner, a middle-aged man with a German accent, strange eyes that flickered and a rather disdainful view of this ignoramus that had been foisted on him. Ignoring my total lack of knowledge he immediately set me to work on some impressively new chemistry involving a new type of plasticiser – chemicals that make plastics malleable, a major focus of Lankro's work. It was only several years later that I appreciated the novelty and seriously advanced chemistry I had been thrown into. Fortunately, Frank helped me out and showed me how to set up flasks and condensers, distil and use a vacuum, do elementary glass-blowing and the myriad of other mysteries that chemistry labs took for granted, most of which were involved in this my first project.

I discovered a great family atmosphere at Lankro; generations of the same family had happily worked there. Amongst them were several keen cyclists and we started to meet at weekends and cycle firstly to Southport and back and later the return trip to Blackpool. We always had time to have a walk, get fish-and-chips and tea before returning home exhilarated.

Outside Dick's Bar, Borrowdale - now part of Lodore Hotel

Blackpool by bike with Frank & Geordie

Lankro dance with Geordie and Arthur - in my Tweed jacket

Climbing on Dovestones

First date - Margaret

At Lankro gates - long after they closed and I retired - with Bob, who died a few days later

Bob and I outside Wall End Barn, Langdale

with Alan in the Cuillins Skye

Tony

Frank

Anne

The Union Ball

First photo with Jean

Alf, I discovered, was a mountaineer, going to the Alps every summer to climb some peak or other.

In fact, Lankro had several experienced rock climbers and mountaineers in its midst, all members of the rather elite Rucksack Club. The star ex-climber was Arthur Birtwhistle, the company treasurer and a legend in the pre-war climbing fraternity. Alf invited me to an annual Beginners Meet of the club, to take place at Laddow Rocks, near Greenfield. Frank and I together with another assistant in the Analytical lab called Bob Buckley, who had done some climbing already, went along and Alf kindly passed on to me an unbelievably ancient pair of boots. They were armed on the soles with Tricounis and heels with Clinkers. These were metal bits nailed on to grip the rock. They rattled and banged as I walked and the boots were rather uncomfortable but they were free!

The overcast day came, a Sunday and I had to do my hostel chores on the Saturday, get up early on Sunday and make my own breakfast and make sandwiches, all most disapproved of by the hostel hierarchy. The first route we tackled was Long

Climb, a Very Difficult. Oooohurhh! I was tied onto the rope having been shown how to tie a bowline and followed Alf who was belayed 30' above me encouraging me on. Wow! I actually enjoyed the experience, even though I slipped off when a Tricouni came away from my left boot and was held tight by Alf. The second 'pitch' continued thereafter and I couldn't wait for another go. After that I was flying and thoroughly enjoyed the day. I met some of the revered senior members, one of whom gave me a back issue of the Rucksack Club Journal. I devoured every word. I recall an article entitled 'Upper Engadine Lowdown' which could well have been referring to the moon, it seemed so remote to my knowledge. One day I'll go there, I thought. That proved to be several decades later. I was hooked. At last I'd found an activity that that I could do and didn't involve balls or athletics. Bob Buckley felt exactly the same and we became bosom pals and determined to continue climbing. It seemed that Clinkers and Tricounis had been replaced long ago with Vibram-soled boots, common on all outdoor boots today, and some of my first pay of about

£125 per year – after passing most of it to the hostel – went on a pair.

My first week also introduced me to the College at Salford when I enrolled and began S1, the first course in Chemistry. The other subjects such as Maths and Physics were a doddle since I had already covered most of the material for O Level but I certainly found the Chemistry tough since it assumed some background school studies. However, after struggling for the first half year and just scraping through the mid-term exams, I blossomed in the second half and passed into my second year with good results. The Lecturers, mostly with Doctor before their names, seemed unbelievably knowledgeable and suggested a remote and impossible level of education from my lowly status.

Before my second year I had been transferred to the Leather Pigments lab under another refugee Dr Levy, an old chap with an impressively beaky nose and a German accent that occasionally was difficult to understand. The work was incredibly dull compared to the research lab, merely matching colours and mixing pigments; Turkey

Red, Alizarin, Prussian Blue and so on. My more experienced colleague, Don, again put me through my paces. After a few months old Levy died and my apprenticeship was switched to work with the Works chief research chemist, Dr John Blakeway, a tall, slim, fit young man, very cheerful and bustling, who rushed from lab to plant and on to the Pilot Plant, where smaller scale plant trials were conducted. This was more like it. He took one look at my slim build and asked me to become cox for his boat at the nearby Agecroft Rowing Club the next Saturday. I declined as I was already committed to join Bob on a visit to Dovestones for some climbing.

We got on well. I recall an occasion when he rushed into the lab with a rather dark sample of the latest batch of DOP from the plant. 'This should be water-white' he said; 'See what you can do with it', at which he disappeared. I tried several tricks used on the plant, washing with alkali, adding charcoal – but with no effect. In desperation I tried washing with ammonia solution and miraculously, the brown colour transferred from the DOP to the ammonia solution. I phoned John and told him. To my amazement – and perhaps horror – he ordered the plant to be loaded with 1000 litres of ammonia, stirred and the mixture separated. Phew! It worked with no hitches and was adopted thereafter. We also had hairy incidents – mostly due to my ignorance or negligence. On one occasion I left the lab on some errand but had left a distillation going. When I returned the whole lab was full of benzene vapour. I rushed in and switched off the heat source, not realising that this could have resulted in an explosion or fire, as well as my being poisoned with the carcinogenic vapours. I - and the lab - survived, fortunately.

Meanwhile back at the hostel I was becoming an irritant. Every weekend I was missing, going climbing and upsetting the protocol. Most of my friends had left and even 'nipper' was now employed in a Manchester pet shop. Also I was getting fed up with the antics of the Old Man, while the busy-bodying Jewish authorities who were again trying to enrol me in a club, the intention of which was for me to end up on a Kibbutz in Israel. I yearned for freedom. Fortunately the Restitution people, urged by my tireless, and as yet unmet, grandfather, had come up with an annual payment to see me through my training and education of £200 per year.

I decided that it was time to leave the hostel after 18 months of riding my bike 14 miles through Manchester traffic every day come rain, snow or shine. Together with Mr Street, I found a lodging with a family in East Didsbury, slightly nearer to Lankro. They were a pleasant family, a Scotsman, one of the 'Ladies from Hell' in the recent war and his wife and daughter of my age but not my fancy. Within a week of moving in I bought a small motorbike from a Lankro colleague, a James 125cc with springing on the front only and very noisy. John Blakeway had given me an old banger which I never managed to get going but this one was perfect. The house was so small! I wasn't used to low ceilings and small, stifling rooms with a coal fire at front and a draught behind. For a few hours I was actually homesick but my first breakfast of cereal, egg and bacon soon changed that.

Returning to Lankro after my summer holiday I discovered that I had been moved once more, this time to the Pilot Plant, still under John Blakeway but directly under Tommy Rhodes. Tommy was an ex-merchant seaman with the sea still very much in his veins. He was a bachelor, but to my surprise not too long after, he married the assistant head of the Analytical laboratory, the Matron, Moira, who more than once had torn a strip off me and from whom I never saw a smile. He longed to return to the sea and on Fridays, once we had tidied up the Plant room, we would sit on drums and he would tell me tails of the sea. After I left Lankro he did indeed go back to being a merchant seaman, but worked on land, finally getting his Captains ticket.

At Christmas time John Blakeway would bring a Christmas pudding wrapped in aluminium foil and tie it to the steam pipes and leave it for days to cook. He told me that when visiting his elderly mother in Shrewsbury, he would wrap a piece of beef and similarly and cook it wired to his sports car's exhaust manifold! Next door to the Pilot Plant was the Engineering workshop, a hotbed of communists and powerful union men. Their leader was Harry Bridge, who, curiously, took a liking to me and we got on well as long as politics wasn't mentioned. He was a big solid chap who often cursed the bosses, management and all in authority, viewing them as oppressing the workers. He was ably assisted by Bernard who had fought in the Spanish Civil War against Franco and was a foul-mouthed, grim character.

At Christmas time we held a works party with everything supplied by the genial Dr 'Krock', food, plenty of drinks and lots of prizes awarded for those who had made contributions to the company's progress. One such prize was awarded to Harry Bridge for his Shop-Stewardship of the engineers. This was a generous gesture, presumably designed to lower the temperature between the engineers and management. However, Harry, with plenty of drink in him, stood up and gave a tirade of bile against Dr Kroch and all his team and the way they ground down the working man. You could have heard a pin drop when he finished. I looked at the embarrassed engineers who stared at the floor in dismay. Dr Kroch rose slowly, walked over to Harry, grabbed him by the collar and frog-marched him out; he took him to the works gate and threw him out telling him not to bother returning. No one objected and peace was restored. The party went on with plenty of jollity thereafter. One of the girls in the office had apparently somehow got hold of a photograph of a Lankro crowd with me on it, had me enlarged and let it be known. The photo went round the lab folks and ended up with me. Red-faced I looked around to find this girl, Margaret, smiling in my direction. I'd never danced before and have two left feet but with her encouragement we danced a bit together and I arranged to see her again, to visit the Palace Theatre in Manchester to see an American pop singer in action. That was the end of the affair, when she and a thousand other girls started screaming all the way through the concert.

On my second summer at Lankro, the cycling gang decided to tour England, staying at youth hostels. Frank from the Analytical lab could not go but urged me to take his super light sports bike for the trip. Four of us, Arthur, another Frank, Billy, a Geordie from the plant and myself set off for Shrewsbury first stop, around 70 miles. It was brilliant and my bike was so fast I couldn't believe how much slicker it was than my own. We took food with us and cooked for ourselves, pancakes being the chief component. They started off being made from eggs, flour and creamy milk –

delicious. Later on the trip as finances dwindled they were just flour and water. The next day we set off for Bath. Hurtling down a hill with me well in front, I turned to see where the others were. In that fraction of a second I veered onto the grass verge and straight into a tree stump in the hedgerow. I shot off my bike, straight over the hedge and landed in a field on all fours, none the worse for the flight. However, my bike bounced right back into the road into the path of Frank who, in avoiding a collision came off heavily onto the rough road surface, badly bruising himself. Arthur proved an effective manager and first patched up Frank, who fortunately had not broken anything and then examined my bike. The front wheel was buckled and crossbar and down tube slightly bent to shorten my wheelbase but otherwise was not badly damaged. He and Billy rode off to the nearest town and returned some time later with a surprisingly straight wheel. Frank, myself and my bike seemed to have got off lightly and we had no other mishaps. At Batheaston Youth Hostel it was a hot evening and we four surreptitiously took our bedding and slept on the verandah. The next day was also glorious warm weather and our ride took us through Bournemouth for lunch and on to Burley in the New Forest. We thoroughly enjoyed the local pub and the local lasses, though the local gentry looked down on us. It wasn't helped by Billy teaching us Geordie songs such as 'Keep yer feet still Geordie Hinnie…' and the 'Blaydon Races', which we sang with gusto.

Next stop was Winchester where the Youth Hostel was an old mill and advertised water-skiing as one of its options. We discovered that a wooden chair seat was attached to an overhead beam, and sat on the rushing mill race. One gingerly lowered oneself onto the seat, clung to a rope and began to ski, slowly becoming more daring with the tricks. Any mistake and you were shot out into the mill pond to the hilarity of the spectators. I fear 'Elf & Safety' would intervene today.

 Slowly we wound our way back north on an increasingly hillier route and all arrived back feeling brilliant. Frank-of-the-bike was none too pleased at his shortened bike and though I offered to pay for a new frame – gulp – he wouldn't hear of it.

At that stage in my Lankro career, Dr Köbner called me in for an interview and looking at my record to date asked me 'Wouldn't you fancy a job of a more physical nature?' He had a friend, Mr Cowhig, in another company, British Celanese, who was seeking a chap like me in his physics laboratory. I assured him that I really wanted to work in Chemistry Research. I also assured him that I was learning fast and had just passed S2 well. He allowed me to return to his laboratory. I was left in the capable hands of the more experienced scientists and enjoyed the work, becoming the lab glassblower into the bargain.

One fine chap I encountered regularly was the Plant Manager, Mr Ken Tomlinson, always smartly turned out with a Clark Gable moustache and pucker accent. Talking to him one day he proffered some advice. 'For much of my working life I needed a supplementary source of income. I started to write short stories, often with a female nom-de-plume and they have appeared in all sorts of magazines, mostly those for woman. The income pays for our holidays and has furnished our house. You ought to find a secondary source of income.' I took his advice to mind but realised for the present there was already plenty on my plate. Years later I instigated the Tomlinson Principle and achieved similar success, though not in short story writing. I also started reading his short stories in Argosy, a magazine of that era.

On my long day and evening at Salford Tech I still occasionally met Feo Scheinman and Bernard Reil, both now in the educational stratosphere from my perspective. Lectures for us lowly types were in several of the outbuildings owned by the College, some in Hankinson (Hanky) Park, the terraced slum area of Salford. The whole College enterprise was managed by a handful of office staff and a dynamic Principal, Peter (later Sir Peter) Venables. He was trained as a chemist, a good beginning, and was a man full of new ideas. He was determined to make something of this back-water Technical College. The College had a long local history dating back to 1852 and served the vast industrial requirements of Manchester in Engineering, Chemistry and other trades. I recall someone walking down a corridor carrying a bucket with a cows head in it. This was part of the Practical work for those working in the food industry. Also a thriving Art School existed on the top floor of the fine 1896 Peel building, the College headquarters. This had been the home of the then still thriving local artist L S Lowry and a collection of his paintings, which were not particularly well visited or respected at that time, were in the adjacent Salford Art Gallery.

Lankro was growing fast and business was booming. Amongst numerous new appointments was a brash new, pipe-smoking Plant Manager, Roger Kingsley, a chemical engineer. He undertook a big expansion programme to the works. Also a new and genial Italian researcher, Dr Molinario, began in my laboratory. He was polite and quietly spoken but very bright. Times were changing and fast.

Early one morning I was walking to the Pilot Plant with some message for Tommy Rhodes when I noticed our large tanker containing concentrated sulphuric acid was surrounded by a pool of what looked to me like sulphuric acid! Had someone left the tap open? I alerted Tommy and we sent an urgent call to Roger, always an early starter. It wasn't the tap but a leak in the cast iron material the tanker was made from! Amazingly, the acid does not dissolve cast iron but creates a protective layer. Dilute sulphuric acid would dissolve the tank furiously. It took months to discover the fault. The tanker sat on several shaped, narrow concrete bases to support it and it appears that a bacterium found a snug, moist home between the concrete and the tanker. It was a bacterium that lived on iron and had moved into a small crack and nibbled its way through.

Bob Buckley and I invested in an old hemp rope that became stiff when wet and some nylon slings and Karabiners and felt like real rock climbers on our first expedition back to Laddow on our own. Taking the bus from Stephenson's square in central Manchester (near 'Nipper's' pet shop) to Greenfield, we tramped across the peat moors to the crag, overlooking the Chew Valley. It didn't strike us as strange that the gritstone rock was blackened from distant smoke from mills; after all the whole of Manchester was black, especially the Town Hall. We tackled all the routes we had done following the Rucksack Club experts with ease and finally tried our hand at some tougher ones – with a top rope. We returned home exhilarated with our stiff rope draped alternately around one or the other's shoulders like a badge of office. In the following weeks we decided we should try out the granite rocks in the Lake District or North Wales, having listened to tails from Alf of his exploits when younger. Bob was a good organiser and had invested in a climbing guide for the Langdale Valley, so on our next opportunity we hitch-hiked to Ambleside, surprisingly easily, on Friday after work and walked the 8 miles down to Wall End Barn beyond The Old Dungeon Ghyll hotel. For a shilling a night, the local farming brothers, Ike and Zeek, allowed climbers to sleep in their straw-covered barn. It proved most comfortable and dry and the camaraderie of the climbers, who spent their evenings in the ODG was great. On the Saturday we climbed on Ravens Crag behind the hotel, finding the sharp handholds and well grooved granite so much more interesting than climbing on the rough and rounded gritstone. Holly Tree Traverse was typical and each route involved 3 or 4 pitches, which made climbing much more challenging. The next day we ascended to Gimmer Crag, a much larger piece of granite and a greater challenge with numerous climbs available at our modest level, before we took the bus to Ambleside and hitched back home feeling smug.

In the following months Bob and I extended our climbing both in location and in difficulty. The breakthrough day came when we were once more back in Langdale and climbing on a large slab called White Ghyll. The climb was our first attempt at a VS – Very Severe – climb, with Bob on the lead. At the crux of the climb Bob froze and just could not tackle the difficult section, returning to my belay ledge. I offered to give it a try. To my delight – and surprise – I found it quite straightforward and soon brought up Bob. From that time on we 'lead through' which implied we tackled alternate pitches, and our climbing ability advanced in leaps and bounds. We explored other crags in Lakeland such as Bowfell and outlying areas such as Eskdale and Wasdale, often walking many miles before climbing.

We next went down to the Llanberis Pass, sleeping under the Cromlech Stones, massive overhanging boulders. I arrived there before Bob one Friday and got out my Primus stove, kettle and a loaf of sliced bread. A stream of clean water was about 20 yards away and returning with a full kettle I observed my last slice of bread disappearing down a rat hole. I sat on top of the stone with a morsel of my precious cake on a stone as bait and a large boulder, but ratty was no doubt snoozing by then or laughing at my ineptitude. We climbed on Dinas Mot and other nearby crags and lived frugally. We also camped in the Ogwen valley, climbing on Tryfan, the Idwal Slabs and their neighbours, generally in pouring rain. We took a tent to Ogwen and camped near the lake, Llynn Ogwen, invariably sited on boggy land.

In winter we tried our hand at climbing frozen waterfalls using ice axes to cut steps and holds, such as Kinder Scout in Derbyshire and one New Year ventured to Glencoe, the bleakest spot in Britain. Despite high snows and ice and low temperatures we rock climbed on Buchel Etive Mor, Bracket & Slab route. That evening, supping beer in the convivial Kingshouse Hotel in front of a blazing fire, our cheerful New Year festivities were interrupted by a gaunt messenger 'There's been an accident on the flanks of Buchel. We need a search party.' Bob and I were one of the few reasonably sober folks there, the Scots having downed quite some whisky. We set off in the pitch dark and perishing cold with stretchers and rescue gear stored at the hotel, using torches to light our way. We discovered that two brothers had been walking on the ridge behind Buchel and were worried at the encroaching darkness. One of them decided to take the short cut down a snow-filled gully. He found, too late that the presumed snow was ice and disappeared rapidly to the bottom. His brother sought in vain and called us out. We eventually found the man, apparently lying on his back waiting for us. His eyes were open when we arrived and we were puzzled why he did not register an interest. When we turned him over he had no back to his head. The walk back was silent and sobering. We never returned to Glencoe.

Meanwhile I had started S3 and really enjoyed Organic Chemistry though I found the Calculus tough. A book by Silvanus P Thompson, FRS – 'Calculus Made Easy' – which I found in Salford Library, came to my rescue. It was the most readable, humorous and enjoyable maths books I had ever come across. I note that it is still in print today, over 60 years later. Our Organic Chemistry lecturer was Donald 'Danny' White, an inspiring man who never used notes. I discovered that the reason was he could not see them with his beer-bottle-bottom glasses. One day in the lab with him he asked me what I intended to do after National Certificate. I presumed that I would continue on part-time to gain a Higher National. He suggested I should apply for a local Council grant to attend full time and study for an ARIC – Associate of the Royal Institute of Chemistry, a degree equivalent open to those with a good National Certificate and told me that he would support my application, given the required results.

In 1954, my final year at Lankro, I was invited by Aunt Dora to join the Meth family reunion that was to take place in Munich that summer. They even bought me a ticket to get there – rail to London, then on to Dover, Belgium and the train to Munich all in 3rd Class, which was a 24 hour journey on wooden seats. Arriving at the Manchester station, the ticket man asked me if I wanted my luggage 'registering'. This seemed a good idea for my one small, battered case – which also contained my sandwiches. I didn't see that case again till Munich! Apart from some water that I begged from a steward that was my food for the trip. Arriving at Munich station I was met by my grandfather, Opa in German, whose English was very limited, together with his brother-in-law Fred Apple, a long-term New York resident, a drawling German-American speaker. They were horrified by my news of having eaten nothing and, having recovered my case, took me off to the station restaurant and ordered a Schnitzel Holstein. Food was still rationed in Britain and limited in quantity. Not so in Germany – an enormous round silver platter arrived which I thought large for the three of us – but this was just for me! In the centre was an enormous Wiener Schnitzel, on top of which was a fried egg. Surrounding this were portions of numerous vegetables and potatoes, roasted, mashed and boiled. Finally on the outside were delicacies which I'd never seen before such as caviar, paté de foie gras and other morsels. I had never before seen such a plateful but like my other relatives, my grandfather decided that I needed some serious feeding up.

When I had gamely managed to eat half of this feast and given up the struggle, they took me to a clothes shop and bought me a new set of clothes, including, to my surprise, a Harris Tweed jacket. It was rather larger than my size but grandfather was intent on ensuring that I soon filled it. All this time he was asking endless questions, using Fred as an interpreter and commenting how he saw aspects of my mother in me. The stay was interesting and enjoyable, especially our visit to the Hofbrauhaus, where, after imbibing a stein of good lager I caused much mirth by trying to get off with a young Münchner Kindl, the girls who delivered fistfuls of steins. Gathered there were my grandparents and Fred, Aunts Friedel from USA and Hertl from Haifa, Israel (in southern Germany it was common to add a diminutive 'el' or 'l' after the name of friends or relatives) as well as Dora and Selma from London. My grandmother, who had waved me off from Ulm station 13 years earlier could not hide her emotions on my rediscovery and how it brought back the tragic memories of her daughter Thea. I learnt how to get around Munich on the tram, getting off at Schiller Denkmal (the statue to their

18th century poet and polymath) and Lehnbach Platz for our hotel, as well as how to get to the Hofbrauhaus, to which I returned alone, becoming good friends with a young German electrician, Gunter who I met there.

More gigantic meals followed. On one occasion Opa ordered a Deutsches Beefsteak for me, an enormous slab of an almost raw fillet of beef. I cut it into strips and asked the waiter in my halting German to cook them well and return the food on a new plate, much to his and my family's horror. Having not long been converted from vegetarianism, raw meat was one step too far. The family were surprised, firstly that I spoke almost no German on arrival and also at the speed at which I picked it up. I can't say that I enjoyed the new Germanic Jewish family environment but found some pleasure in the trip and got on well with my new growing circle of Meths. They pressed me to emigrate to USA or Israel but that was the furthest thing on my mind. However, I did promise to give my grandparents a visit in St Petersberg, Florida. Opa upgraded my return journey to 2nd Class and pressed some dollars and Deutschmarks into my hand and my return to

England proved happier than my outward journey. Little did I know that this was my first and last occasion I would see my grandfather.

Chapter 6

Nearly a graduate, nearly a murderer

The possibility of a full time education gave me the incentive to work sufficiently hard to achieve the required grades and I was offered a place on the ARIC course and a grant of £220 per year. The net result was that on leaving Lankro in1954 to go full time to Salford Tech, I was no worse off than when I was working. I also decided to move nearer to the College and before starting, went to live in Eccles, not far from Lankro, lodging with Mr and Mrs Spencer and their two young schoolboys. Mr Spencer was a highly intelligent man who worked in the centre of Manchester and we got on well. He obviously needed someone else to converse with since he and his German wife – they were married when he was on army service in Germany after the war - were decidedly living separate existences. I kept totally neutral in the matter. However, Mrs Spencer had other ideas and it slowly dawned on me that she was trying her best to get me into her bed. When I came down for breakfast, all the males having left for work or school, she would serve me topless except for a bra. I ignored all her attempts, at first thinking it was a huge joke. When things got more pointedly overt I decided reluctantly that I had to leave. There was no way I could discuss the matter with Mr Spencer and she wouldn't take no for an answer.

After my first month at the College I found a nearby top-floor two-room flat in a very smart corner of Eccles in the home of Mr and Mrs Lord, a local potato-crisp-making company owner. Now I was on my own, cooking and caring for myself. I had a small gas stove and bought a pressure cooker, which allowed me to put in all the ingredients for a meal. I soon became quite proficient at following the accompanying recipe book. Nearby was a Polish grocery shop and they always had something interesting, different – and cheap. My best discovery was red cabbage, cooked piquant; one cabbage made quite a number of portions and was great with sausages and potatoes. As there were three apartments on our top floor I also had friends there, one of whom worked in the offices at Lankro. She had a boyfriend, with whom she made rather loud sex. Mrs Lord was pregnant with their third child and one day, working at home on some chemistry, she called up to me to come down, where a cup of tea was waiting. She informed me that she had started to be 'in labour' which conveyed nothing to me except something was not quite normal as she was looking uncomfortable. She explained with a laugh that the baby was on its way but not sure when! I remember from my Scala cinema days that people boiled water and collected towels, which I suggested red-facedly to her. Again she laughed and then winced. No, she just wanted me to be available until her husband returned in a few hours. The thought of having to deliver a baby was a pretty unnerving one. However, when she called me down again she explained that the midwife was coming and I could relax. I got dressed and got on my motorbike to go to Salford Library. Phew! The baby arrived that night with no complications and little fuss.

A young chap, David, took the next door flat when the Lankro lady left. He told me he had just started working in a shoe shop in Eccles. At that time I was saving up sixpenny pieces in a milk bottle on my fireplace, which also occasionally held a shilling by mistake. These were for my gas and electricity meters. One evening returning from Salford I noticed the shilling wasn't on top as it had been. I was not in the habit of locking my door and immediately thought it might be David so the following afternoon I returned early and hid behind the corner curtain that contained my hung clothes. Just as I expected, David arrived not too long after, knocked on my door and with no response, entered, picked up the milk bottle and as he was pouring out some money, I came out saying 'OK, you can give me that'. He collapsed into my armchair white-faced. I suggested that he owed me at least as much again as he took out and he agreed, profusely apologising, telling me that he was really broke, had been thrown out of his home, his parents hated him and he would never do it again. It happened that the Lords were away and I was left in charge, especially to feed and walk their large Alsatian dog. I walked him that morning early and left for College, having arranged for David to feed the dog on returning home as I would be late. When I returned home the dog nearly ate me. I fed the hungry animal and went upstairs to find that not only was David not there but he had emptied the room even of anything removable belonging to the Lords, and left. I found an envelope in the bin with his name and another address on it, found the phone number in the phone book and spoke to a weeping mother who told me of the criminal behaviour of their son. She had no idea where he was so I phoned the police. The first thing they noticed on entering his room was that he had emptied both the gas and electricity meters. They knew all about him and soon caught him attempting another burglary. Fortunately the dog had protected the Lord's residence area.

The room was later occupied by a smart city man called John and we got on really well. He enjoyed a hearty breakfast and we had a spell where we alternately made breakfast. Inevitably it became a little competitive and we would try to introduce novel features into the menu. I consulted my friendly Polish shop lady to get new ideas and often had a special loaf of bread or served up a (then rare) pink grapefruit to add some zing. Sadly he left all too soon, but it improved my culinary skills – and table manners, he being a napkin man.

Next door to the Lords was a large detached house with a lonely widow as the sole occupant. She was decidedly suspicious of a young, motor-biking student called Otto living next door and told Mrs Lord her feelings. I had already learnt to switch off my noisy, two-stroke engine on getting near the flat and would cruise in to the Lords so as not to annoy her. She spent much of her time peeping out of her curtains checking on me. One day I got another student friend, David Humphries, to ride the unsprung pillion on my bike and on this occasion I kept the engine going. He got off, I took a spade from the shed and dug a hole in the garden and David furtively took a box from his pocket and put it in the hole. I covered it up and we looked in all directions and drove off again. Mrs Lord thought the whole incident hilarious when contacted by the local constabulary, who had become well acquainted with dear old Mrs Stevenson. The box was ceremoniously dug up and the contents were a piece of paper with 'Boo!' written on it. I later got on quite well with Mrs Stevenson, even buying a strip of carpet from her for my flat.

The ARIC course was a big surprise. It comprised 3 days of practical work, mainly housed in the vast, Paddington-Station-like laboratory, C22, in the 1896 Peel building. This lab could house over 100 students easily and had an immensely high ceiling with semi-circular steel girders supporting it. Smells disappeared upwards. At the far end was an immense long raised bench, behind which sat several staff members looking after their particular group of students. We were each given a bench, locker and basic equipment and were required to keep them in good order. A jovial storeman, Norman, and his assistant Mary were the life and soul of the place. I enjoyed my stints in the lab and seemed to take to most of the work with gusto. That is except for Quantitative Gravimetric Analysis, to me a pointless venture. It required using some very tricky scales weighing in grams to 5 places of decimals, and getting the wretched balance to stop swinging about was a pain. I had no patience with it.

Lectures comprised Organic Chemistry with Danny White, Physical Chemistry with a different lecturer every month or two and Inorganic Chemistry which was also somewhat chaotic. We also studied Maths, Physics, Physiology and Technical German and later Technical Russian, the last two designed to allow us to consult the chemical literature in these languages. The latter proved useful in that I would label all my solvent bottles in Russian to minimise theft. I soon realised that my passion was for organic chemistry which I absorbed like a sponge. This is the chemistry of carbon compounds and thus the chemistry of life. However, full time education also meant full time freedom and there were plenty of distractions for a young chap freshly released from the confines of institutional life. I had some catching up to do, and I didn't waste time. Our bunch of about 50 students was an excellent variety of souls. Tony Mackie and a few others had just finished their National Service, in Tony's case in the Air Force, so were more mature and experienced in life. The majority had followed my route, often as late developers, some having failed 11 plus and worked hard, studying part-time to make up the entry requirements. Others had come straight through the grammar school system, gained A level chemistry but for one reason or another had chosen ARIC rather than a degree at a traditional

University. Usually they had not all the requirements for a University degree course, maybe lacking a foreign language qualification. With others, the reason was family importunity and living at home allowed them to get a higher education. It was possible to study at Salford for an external London University degree, as was the case with Feo, and my old Lankro colleague, Frank Brimelow. However, this required the appropriate A levels. Despite their poor start in life the majority went on to excel. ARIC was beginning to become a respected degree equivalent in the workplace and even for doctorate entry, though the snootocracy still regarded it as a poor second to a 'proper' degree.

I quickly discovered the Students Union and that cash was available to start new activity groups and in no time I had started the Royal Salford Mountaineering Group together with finance for equipment. On the next occasion Bob – still at Lankro – and I went climbing, I sported a smart new nylon rope, with new slings and karabiners. We were in the pink and Tony, Frank Brimelow and Alan Hubbard, an engineer, soon joined our gang. We ventured to Borrowdale on our first

College trip after some training for the newer recruits on gritstone. Camping by Derwentwater, we climbed on Shepherds Crag, just yards from the road and in the evenings enjoyed the convivial atmosphere at Dicks Bar, sadly no longer there but incorporated into the upmarket Lodore Hotel.

The Head of chemistry was Dr Edwards, 'red Ted' to us because of his political inclinations, his assistant being the genial inorganic chemist, Albert Taylor. I recall Albert often getting side-tracked with anecdotes, always more interesting than his lectures. On one occasion he told us about the discovery of fluorocarbons, which were the universal refrigerants in use then. He told us of their first preparation and their totally boring stability. They were unreactive, non-inflammable and inert and were almost ignored, until their refrigerant properties were discovered. Everything has its use, he reminded us. Little did he know then that they were the scourge of the ozone layer that protects the earth from UV irradiation and would in time be banned.

Times were changing fast. A new Head of chemistry arrived, Dr George Rowntree Ramage, the ex-head of chemistry at Huddersfield Tech. He was from Hartlepool, with a broad north-eastern accent, calling everyone 'laddie' and beginning many a sentence with 'whatistacallit'. He was tall, always wore black boots and had one glass eye. He had a curious fear of spending pence but could spend thousands without batting an eyelid. He once bought a job lot of junk from the closing Woolwich Arsenal which meant that we had to suffer using very brittle, pre-war test tubes in the lab for a year or more until they were all broken. We were also landed with half a ton of amyl salicylate, a chemical with no use to man, which appeared in many lab practical examinations for a year before it was quietly sent to an incinerator.

Chemistry was booming in the greater Manchester area. Many large companies such as ICI with its many divisions, Geigy, Clayton Aniline and numerous others employed thousands. Three of the largest chemistry departments in Britain were just a few miles apart, Manchester University, UMIST and Salford. However, on the research front Salford was a midget and Ramage was determined to change that. He brought 6 of his PhD students with him to add to the handful of those already present, one being Feo. The research laboratory accommodation and equipment was primitive, a joke really, and Ramage appointed several new research-minded new staff, including Dr Hans Suschitzky, an Austrian refugee organic chemist. However, research was still run on a shoestring budget.

Tony Mackie's father was a doctor in Eccles, not far from my residence, and his wife was a cheerful soul who spent much of her time smoking and drinking, but took me in as if I was still an orphan. I was often invited for a meal and parties at Tony's became a big event with no shortage of drink and food. They tended to have upper crust friends with smart sports cars and money, but I seemed to be tolerated cheerfully. On one occasion at a party a group were discussing some aspect of motor racing. I listened but said nothing until one of them asked me what I did. Maybe the beer was at work because I told them I worked in the research department near Brands Hatch, a motor racing circuit. We did contract research for racing car companies. They were all intrigued, asking me what in particular I did. Of course I could not go into detail but my present research involved valve bounce in high revving engines. I really convinced these chaps, who were agog at hearing the hottest work determining the next advance in speed. I never discovered if I had got away with my tale but it got me into the 'club'.

My first mid-term examinations at Christmas time were a shock in that I had clearly spent too much time on other activities. I began to realise what every student has to recognise at some time; that 'understanding' and 'remembering' were two totally different matters. I had to pull my socks up. I found Physical Chemistry tough as it involved quite some high level maths and strange concepts. On one occasion Dr Kingston was lecturing on the famous Schrödinger equation, in a grand old Victorian lecture theatre with tiered seats and a large demonstration bench in the front. Several large roller blackboards were on the wall behind him. He was an amazing chap with a very lopsided head, no notes and was totally ambidextrous. He would start at the left side of the first blackboard with his left hand, switching to his right when he arrived at the right side. He had filled several boards full of complex maths, line after line and suddenly stopped, stood back and scratched his head. The room was quiet as we all paused in our note taking. Suddenly, the quiet voice of Andrew Whittaker piped up and said 'I think you made a mistake 9 lines up' and continued to explain the error in detail. To the amazement of all of us, who had not followed anything of the maths but just recorded the information, he was right. He went on later to get a PhD in Physical Chemistry.

Ramage lectured to us in one of the out-buildings, an old church hall with pillars. I recall he walked straight into one on his glass eye side but didn't stop for a moment in his lecture. David Dollimore was a boring lecturer of physical chemistry, totally dependent upon his notes. When he turned to the board, one of the wags would shuffle his notes and leave poor old David baffled. David was a 'Surface Chemist' his research involved studying the adsorption of gases onto solids and involved complex glassware much of it filled with columns of mercury. I recall that his rough wooden floors were spattered with mercury droplets. Nobody seemed any worse off for the potential poisoning and I still know one of his co-workers. 'Onkle' Hans Suschitzky lectured us on Heterocyclic chemistry, concerning products near to those of nature and was genial and enjoyable. Dr Holt's speciality was sugar chemistry and a long running banter sprinkled liberally with jokes ran between lecturer and students, which he would carry on at the next lecture. When he arrived one day there was a large structure drawn on the blackboard of a complex sugar that also had a likeness to him. All sugars have names ending in –ose, such as glucose. This one was called Holtose. He enjoyed it and made a difficult and potentially boring subject interesting. Our Technical German lecturer was a very large, well-spoken gentleman who had the unfortunate habit of dozing off mid-lecture. Fortunately he was aware of the problem and always gave us something to translate when he arrived so we did not miss too much. To my surprise, German came easily.

That first summer break I obtained a vacation job at Burtonwood Airbase, an American air force base. The man who employed us had bought the contract for all the scrap metal from the site. Our job, armed with a typical set of burglar's tools, was to chop up old aeroplanes into pieces such that they could be loaded onto railway trucks. All the aluminium was put in one set of wagons, iron and steel in another and other, non-ferrous metals in a third. A key item in our kit was a magnet. We worked long days with short breaks as the contract was strictly time-limited. I still didn't develop muscles but I knew I had worked hard by the end of a month of it.

With the money earned, Frank Brimelow and I decided to hitch hike to the South of France. We hiked separately and arranged to meet firstly in St James Park, London, then in Montmartre, Paris and then in the youth hostel on Ile de St Marguerite, off Cannes harbour. It was a prison island famous for imprisoning the Man in the Iron Mask, made famous by Alexander Dumas. The prison was now a youth hostel. In fact we both turned up in London within an hour of each other and in the evening made a bit of a tent from deck-chairs in St James Park and slept the night, being totally ignored next morning by the bowler-hatted gentry going off to the city. We travelled on to Paris and arrived within half a day of each other but that was no problem. It was amazing how long one could make a cup of coffee last and the living cabaret around one was enthralling. On the way south I was given a lift in a very smart Mercedes driven by a German shipping magnate from Hamburg called Helmut. We swapped stories on the long journey south. He spoke excellent English, having been a student in Oxford before the war. While there he had become good friends with an English student, Brian and they visited each other and kept in touch. On the outbreak of war they both joined up into their respective armies. Helmut was captured early in the war and taken to a UK prisoner-of-war camp. To his surprise the camp commander was his old friend. The soldiers were taken out in work parties to help out nearby farmers and whenever it was possible, he would be picked up by Brian and they briefly resumed their friendship. He was mortified at my war experience, bought me a fine lunch and wanted Frank and I to visit him in his Cannes apartment. I decided that was one step too far but we left with Anglo-German relations somewhat improved. I arrived on the island a day before Frank and we had a great holiday. I made a fatal error. I wrote a postcard to Ramage apologising in case I was late for the start of term, not knowing how long the return trip would take. He thought it the height of cheek and I had a black mark against my name when I missed the first two days of the new term.

Rock-climbing was progressing and Bob and I were now more regularly tackling, and enjoying, hard climbs. We decided that perhaps it was time to visit the climber's Mecca, Cloggy. We camped again under the Cromlech Stones and next morning set off. More correctly the crag is called Clogwyn d'ur Ardu – the very black cliff, a massive piece of rock, split into two buttresses, the east and west, in places over 600' high. In many places it was vertical or even overhanging, being on the flank of Snowdon, not too far from the half-way station of the railway up the mountain. In those days a lovely old lady called Mrs Evans had a café at the halfway house with excellent tea and cakes. The most famous climb was The Great Slab, 600' of solid granite and Very Severe in grade. We loved it and climbed in 'pumps' – tennis shoes - instead of boots. I remember standing high up on a small ledge, being utterly enthralled by the sight and the exposure. We also made acquaintance of the legendary Mancunians, Joe Brown and Don Whillans with their Rock & Ice Club colleagues that weekend. Being slight in stature but reasonably fit I found physically tough climbs easier than did the big solid climbers and shot up the hard and vertical first pitch of the VS, Curving Crack with no problem. It was a narrow, vertical crack that I could hold on the near edge of and put my feet on the far side and 'lay-back', effectively walking up it. When my colleagues couldn't manage it I reversed it and did it again. Only then did I realise the benefit of a light build.

While on Cloggy, we noticed a sheep, high up on a long, grassy ledge. It could only have fallen to get to this airy site, but seemed no worse and was contentedly eating the grass, oblivious to the impossibility of escape. Two weeks later it was still there, looking forlorn and with no grass remaining. I decided that we needed to rescue it and Bob ably supported my endeavours as I climbed firstly above and on the far side of the ledge and slowly descended to it, my pockets filled with grass and a spare lassoing rope around my neck. Little by little I edged towards the sheep offering tempting nibbles, with no positive effect. I made grass parcels and threw them near to the sheep, which half-heartedly took the nearest bits but always backed-away if I came too close. After ages in this crazy cabaret I was out of grass and no nearer a rescue. My lasso attempts were pathetic and only caused the sheep to back ever nearer to the end of the ledge. At last I decided on one last attempt. I tried out my lassoing in the opposite direction as a practice and then, suddenly turned and hurled my noose towards the sheep. It landed well but the sheep wriggled free – and dropped to its death 200' below. I felt terrible as I descended once more to Bob. Weeks later we learnt at the local pub in Bethesda that some idiot had tried to rescue a sheep on Cloggy. The local shepherds wait until the sheep can't move and then are lowered on ropes and rescue the animal. This can be weeks since the sheep even start eating their own wool. They are great survivors it seems.

Other less strenuous activities also started to take up my chemistry time, such as the regular dances that took place at Manchester University Students Union. My dancing ability was abysmal but it was the best place to meet the fairer sex and to have a night out with colleagues and friends. We even occasionally went to the Plaza or Ritz ballrooms in Manchester the latter of which had a certain

Jimmy Savile as manager. These dances changed the course of my life but you will have to wait a bit for the details.

Meanwhile at Salford Tech a meeting was called by the Principal and the Great Hall was packed. He firstly announced that we were selected by Harold Wilson's government to become a College of Advanced Technology, one of eight in the country; and he then outlined the expansion plans for the College. An enormous hole would be dug next to the River Irwell as phase one. It would then be filled in – phase 2, and a new multi-storey building erected to house primarily Chemistry, Physics and Electrical Engineering courses, phase 3. Student numbers would mushroom. We would become one of the major providers of engineers and chemists in the land. The new College would provide its own degree courses instead of external ones and of the eight such colleges we would be the largest. To celebrate the change our year created the 'ARIC 2 '56 Society', with Danny White as its president and socialising and drinking as its primary purpose. I still have the engraved tankard. Instead of a handful of secretaries a new Administration Department was formed and under the direction of Mr Sharman eventually became the largest unit in the College. Such is the way of administrators.

That summer vacation, after passing my examinations, I took a job in a 'Pea Viner' gang near Southport. We were bussed out each day to the facility to which farmers brought their harvest of pea plants complete on hay trailers. Two of us loaded the peas into a hopper with pitch forks, two more operated the pea separator and ensured all went smoothly, two dealt with the silage and two collected the peas in large trays and loaded them onto a trailer. One extra hand drove the tractor, collecting and delivering. This was a 24 hour routine and we did 12 hour shifts. If all went well we might have an hour or two to snooze. For three weeks it was sleep, eat and work with no time for anything else. But the pay was good and following this, Bob and I together with Alan Hubbard set off for the Isle of Skye to climb in the Cuillins in Glen Brittle. This was rough gabbro rock, a cross between granite and gritstone from a climbing viewpoint. We stayed in a B&B with the inevitable Mrs MacDonald for three weeks in weather largely comprised of deluge with occasional bright interludes. I recall that the heavy rain resulted in a river rushing through the house front gate, dividing round the house and the streams re-joining to go out of the back gate. We climbed much of the Cuillin Ridge, culminating in traversing a daunting string of peaks, crossing the highest, Sgurr Alasdair, and ending on Sgurr nan Gilean, from the top of which we could see the last bus setting off from Portree in the north to take us back to Glen Brittle. We ran down to Sligachan to meet it – and missed it by a whisker. After a refreshing drink at the Sligachan Hotel, the 8 mile walk back over the Bealach a' Mhaim (pass of the cattle) was not the easiest of returns. I also recall being on one of the three triangular peaks that made up Sgurr na Madaidh (pronounced Varty! – peak of the foxes) when the mist descended. We had no idea which peak we were on and the compass needle gently circled as it was raised or lowered due to magnetic rock. A long, anxious wait was required before we could see which steep line led safely off the peak. One afternoon, bored with three days of monsoon, we set off in vests and shorts and ran to the youth hostel a couple of miles away for some light relief.

After five seconds we were soaked and after that it was no big issue. Steaming cups of cocoa soon set us up for the return soaking. One highlight of our stay was to race down from the top of the highest peak, Sgurr Alasdair, down the scree slope. One could take giant leaps, a bit like skiing, and were down in minutes.

Not long after these adventures I discovered that Tony Mackie had been evacuated to Blackpool during the war and while there found a service revolver and ammunition on the beach. While shooting at tin cans with his air rifle we decided to try out the revolver, which he had kept hidden at home and never dared to use. We went to Langdale in the Lakes and on a cool, grim day with mist, rain and wind decided to walk up remote Mickelden, up the Rossett Ghyll and then into the wilderness country towards Langstrathdale. We met nobody the whole way and decided that this was the perfect place to try out the revolver. We tossed for who should fire it and I won, much to Tony's relief. I loaded a bullet into the old, heavy gun, held it at arm's length and pulled the trigger, aiming at a rock some distance away. An enormous bang, a massive kick and a blast of cordite resulted, together with a pinging noise of the bullet hitting something. It was an awful experience. What made it worse was the sight of a distant figure wandering in the mist towards Langstrathdale on the far side of the dip we were in, several hundred yards away. Had I hit him? We were convinced that he was walking with difficulty. Was it the wind in his face? Or a bullet? We were horrified as we watched the figure disappear into the mist. That evening, in the Old Dungeon Ghyll bar we talked to Sid Cross about the terrible weather and hoped there had been no fell accidents. None that he knew about, he countered. We kept an eye on the news for the next week or two, hearing a report that Zeek was up looking for a problem sheep and some idiot was firing a gun up Rossett Ghyll way. Phew! Tony handed in the gun at the next amnesty opportunity.

The third year of the ARIC course was tightly packed and even required some evening courses. The final practical examination was to be a 4-day event at Imperial College, London and the written exams could comprise anything on our syllabus or not, this still being an external qualification. Our numbers for the final year had more than doubled with folks arriving from other courses and even from other colleges. Salford was *the* place to obtain an ARIC and employment options thereafter were many. Work for graduates was easy to find in the burgeoning chemical industry and there were plenty of PhD options, particularly abroad. UK Universities were still a bit snooty about accepting non-Bachelor degrees but that was soon to change.

Around this time I was much interested in the eternal questions that must trouble every sentient soul: is there a God? If so, is God interested in mere earthlings? What happens after death? We students often debated these issues but were soon diverted by the attractions of youth. Maybe the deeply instilled – and subsequently buried - moral views of the Ware family were coming to the surface of my mind. One thing I was already convinced of was that all the weird rituals of established religions that I had witnessed to date was more to do with their long history rather than a link to God, if indeed there was one. I wanted no part of mumbo jumbo, having had more than enough in my institutional life.

But a much greater interest was in a girl that I met at a Union dance. I had met her sister, Iris, several times, a stunning raven-haired copy of the young Elizabeth Taylor. She was only interested in the flashy boys and that I was not. However, her sister was a beautiful and happy girl, always with a beaming smile. My fellow ARIC student, Brian Rushton (years later to become President of The American Chemical Society) and I had a bet who could get a date with her, and sadly, I lost. However, I did dance with her and discovered she was called Jean. Brian's date proved a one off so I pursued Jean and managed to secure a date also. At that time the price of a haircut had risen dramatically from 3d to 6d and I had decided that the simple solution was to have my hair cut half as often. So it was as a long-haired student that I first went out with Jean. Salford had started a thriving Gas Engineering course, following the discovery of North Sea gas which replaced coal gas. These students were a lively lot and the day after my date they grabbed me in the Student Union house, tied me to a chair and gave me a rough crew cut - for free. So it was a totally different lad that turned up for the second date. Phew! She thought the whole business was hilarious and joined me at a riotous party the following weekend at Tony Mackie's house. I remember at one stage she was going around in her pencil slim pink skirt wearing a top hat and laughing a lot. That party seemed to cement our relationship and furthermore Mother Mackie approved. I also recall inviting her for a meal in my flat and proudly making dinner including my speciality, piquant red cabbage. As she could barely boil an egg at that time she was impressed. She was a bacteriological technician at Manchester University, working on TB research with Prof Maitland, a well-known specialist in the field. He was also a keen painter and a great friend of L S Lowry, who would occasionally visit the lab. She lived not far from the University and I soon became acquainted with the family, who ran a corner shop selling everything, particularly to the Irish labourers who lived in the neighbourhood and worked on the roads, who also frequented the adjacent pub. They spent bountifully, each week buying a new vest, underpants, handkerchief and fags. Their children were given obscene amounts to use for sweets, and would sit on the pub steps awaiting their inebriated parents. More than once I and Jean's young brother Roy would pick up a stoned Irishman lying on her doorstep and dump him into an 'Irish house' across the road. I enjoyed the occasional hour serving behind their counter with her disabled father who suffered emphysema from long years spent working in the Lancashire cotton mills.

Jean also joined me on rock-climbing jaunts, sporting brand new boots and getting out into the Lake District for the first time. It always amazes me the lengths partners will go to fit in with the foibles of their mate. While she really enjoyed the stunning Lakeland scenery and walking in the hills, I think she no more than put up with the rock bit. She certainly amazed her mother, who presumed her only interest was dancing at that time, and concluded this must be serious.

A final trip to the Lakes and North Wales before serious study for finals beckoned. Having read the guide books I fancied trying a hard VS called Piggott's route on Cloggy and Munich Climb on Tryfan and Bob was more than happy to let me lead them. The first ascent of Munich Climb was by some young Germans, members of the master race, just before the last war, to show the dominance of the Aryan culture. It is a great classic route and a hard VS but pity about the arrogance. I found it an exhilarating experience. Bob was unavailable for the Lakes trip and I took a promising young engineer friend of Alan Hubbard called Joe Smith, a small but tough young chap, new to climbing. I took him on a mild VS route, much harder than anything he had done before, named Bilberry Buttress, a classic climb on Raven Crag. It comprised of three pitches, each with a broad ledge between covered in bilberries. He romped up it and I was impressed. On the way down we passed a short but tough VS called Kneewrecker Chimney. Joe was keen to give it a try and to my surprise climbed over the crux with ease and then returned back down to me! I had struggled with this climb before and did not want to display my lesser ability. I was not surprised to hear that within a couple of months he was a star climbing pal of Joe Brown and Don Whillans, who christened him Morty. He had a great career climbing with them until he suffered a motorbike accident.

The Cloggy trip was very eventful. Firstly, while climbing on Dinas Mot in the Llanberis Pass, Bob and I had to rescue a climber attempting the fierce Diagonal Route, first ascended by the Lankro whizz kid, Arthur Birtwhistle. I also climbed on that occasion with Joe Brown and Don Whillans on another tough route called North-West Arete. But the real target was Piggott's on Cloggy. The first few pitches were straight-forward until I arrived at the crux of the climb. This involved a horizontal traverse under an overhang until I came to a 10' crack that ascended vertically to a narrow ledge. At the bottom of the crack was a pebble stuck in the crack – a 'chockstone' to climbers, but which moved easily as I put a 'runner' – a sling of rope – around it as a safety precaution. I attempted this crack - referred to as The 10' Corner – several times and in different ways with no success. One more try, I decided, but found my weakened muscles just could not handle it and I shouted to Bob to hold tight, I was coming off. Amazingly, the chockstone held me and I was left dangling over an overhang several hundred feet from the ground. I had to climb back up the overhang, remove the sling and return to

Bob, as hard a climb as any to date. Although I impressed a watching friend, Ronny Cummerford, with my parabolic descent and return, I was a decidedly more sober climber from then on. It is worth mentioning that in today's world a climber would insert his own metal 'chockstone' at the top of the crack and even use the attached sling to step up to the shelf. It may be safer but loses something of the original excitement. In fact, as Jean and I became more of an item, my climbing took less and less of my energies. I had several serious steps to take, with impending finals, my new love and my interest in things spiritual.

Chapter 7

Nearly a Christian graduate chemist

I suppose it was David Humphries who persuaded me to take up Christianity. He was a small chap with beer-bottle glasses and a quiet but jovial manner generally. He did not join us in partying and the usual wild student activities. He was taking the external London degree in chemistry so I tended to see him less often. However, we got on well and his sharp wit and telling responses to my queries made me wonder if perhaps there was a less mumbo-jumbo sort of belief possible. Looking back, my endeavour to follow this track probably was a mixed blessing. I found a sort of faith that made some sense at the time but I had to close my mind to large areas of plain common sense, revealed from my studies, that clearly militated against these faith matters. I started to read the bible and despite all the strange and contradictory indications of the nature of God and man revealed therein, I had found something that filled a deep-seated need at the time. The latter allowed me to ignore the numerous and obvious contradictions, ancient but impossible stories and errors. It's easy to become blinkered if you really want to! It took me another couple of decades to untangle the web that I had become caught in. Most believers are brain-washed from birth which is a tough web to escape from. Those who take up religion in later life, especially if they study science subjects, need a strong, ostrich mentality or an even stronger need for a life system that allows them to overcome the logical arguments that today keep most educated people away from active religion. Enough philosophising, but the effect was definitely a damper on the next good few years of my life and that of my kith and kin.

I went along to David's 'church' one day and found it refreshingly simple and lacking in the usual historical baggage. It was a Plymouth Brethren chapel, but despite this dubious connotation was friendly and had real fellowship of believers who took the bible seriously and endeavoured to follow its precepts. It seemed to fill the void in my life at the time and I threw my lot into that group and their version of Christianity, immersion baptism and all. Apparently I'd been 'born again', though I did not recall any 'Road to Damascus' experience.

With Mr Spencer and sons

With the students & staff on the steps of Salford Tech - Danny white 5th from right; me at right

Frank, Tony, Anne & me at party at Tony's

The new chemistry building of Salford University

Tony climbing in Borrowdale

Tony & me at Degree Ball

The large laboratory - our year me - 5th from left

Meanwhile Jean and I discussed the idea of getting married while I was still a student. After all, she could care for me while studying for my finals and two could live as cheaply as one in our young minds. We were walking to my Eccles flat when suddenly Jean coughed – and out came deep-red blood. We were not far from the Mackie household and I took her straight there. Dr Mackie took her immediately to the nearby Hope Hospital in Salford and soon after, TB was diagnosed. Her boss who worked solely on TB research had omitted to give Jean a BCG test (which indicates ones liability to catch TB). She spent a week there before being transferred to Baguley TB Sanatorium. While at Hope Hospital, her boss, Prof Maitland came to visit her, together with his friend, the now-famous painter, L S Lowry. Jean suggested to Lowry to paint the Salford scene out of her window. He stared for a minute and then said in his broad Lancashire accent 'Nay lass, too many trees'.

Jean was in the Sanatorium for over 6 months. I visited regularly on my little James 125cc motorbike and she would save me some of the over-abundance of food she enjoyed. I regularly went home with an egg or two and other goodies. We were poor but very happy and looked forward to her coming out and us getting married. We had some unexpected good news. Jean's mother had been left her mother's house in Blackpool in her will and offered to let us rent it on getting married. The air of Blackpool would be good for her recuperation rather than that of smoggy Manchester. Furthermore, I had been offered a place in Dr Suschitzky's lab to do some research for a higher degree if I successfully graduated, with a grant of the princely sum of £500 per annum, wealth beyond imagining.

Jean recovered well from TB in the course of time. Not too long after her recovery we did indeed get married in snowy January, 1958. The day before the wedding I took the train to Blackpool, got the house ready for our arrival with food and fuel, a fire laid in the grate and some basic furniture that we had bought second hand – a bed and linen, table and chairs etc, though the floors were bare wood. On arrival back in Manchester I picked up my motorbike and was driving back to my Eccles flat. The snow was still thick on the pavements but melting and council workers were shovelling it into the road for the traffic to melt. Just as I arrived, passing Salford Station, a large pile was thrown in my path. The lorry ahead put his breaks on firmly and I did an impressive sideways snowboarding imitation, ending soaking wet in the gutter. My poor old bike had a right-angled handlebar and the chain came off but I was cushioned by the snow and only my pride dampened. I parked it by the station entrance and nipped on a bus back to Jean's place, borrowed some pants from her dad and took the bus to Eccles, having things to attend to before the big day.

The quiet wedding went well and the kind church folk gave us lots of 'kitchen' presents to get us going in Blackpool. Dave was my best man and escorted us to Victoria station for the train to our 'honeymoon' in our new house in Blackpool. As the train was leaving I suddenly remembered my bike! Dave ran along with the train as I told him the story and where it was.

We had a blissful week in our own minimalist home and appreciated the neighbours who cleared the snow from our short drive so that I could carry Jean over the threshold. The small spare bedroom became my study with a large, ancient table and chair filling the space. Jean learned the kitchen arts fast and tried her hand at using the washroom shed in the back which incorporated a copper boiler and corrugated washboard. Washdays were a pain and we soon invested in a second hand top-loading Hoover washing machine which incorporated a mangle to dry off the clothes, which was my job. We felt very with-it when we sold the boiler to a very grateful rag-and-bone man and made the washroom into a garden shed. I managed to scrape up enough cash to buy a season ticket for the then fast train service of one hour to Manchester, resorting to a push bike to the station and alighting at Salford station for the walk to the college.

Returning to Manchester, I asked Dave about my poor, abandoned motor-bike. He told me of his failed endeavours to find it and his visit to Salford Police Station to report the loss. It appears that the police removed the bike and, hearing the circumstances, wedding and all, had fully repaired the bike and gave it back to me with their wedding greetings!

Finals included a four day practical examination in London Imperial College labs. I thoroughly enjoyed the challenge and only discovered years later that I came top in the country. It was my black mark that caused Ramage to withhold the information. We stayed in cheap student lodgings in Cromwell Road and Dave Humphries and I spent an evening on soap boxes at Hyde Park corner, berating the crowds with an off-the-cuff Christian message. We were probably not very effective but it was great fun.

Chapter 8

Nearly a doctoral chemist

Finals were successfully accomplished and I looked forward to getting involved with research for a higher degree. However, there was a problem. The Royal College of Advanced Technology, Salford did not have the ability to award doctorate degrees directly and ARIC was not deemed valid to sign on for an external London University PhD. The new vice-chancellor, who in my experience was somewhat of a buffoon (on one occasion I was in a lift going from the ground floor to the eighth when he walked in, pressed all the buttons and alighted at the first floor!), called Clifford Whitworth, recommended me to take on a newly instituted research diploma in technology that no one had ever heard of. I chose instead to go for another newly created Diploma of Research of The Royal Institute of Chemistry, a 3 year supposed equivalent of a PhD. Prince Philip became our Chancellor and was outstanding at the job. He never used notes but gave brilliant, humorous and student-orientated speeches. He hated protocol, unlike Whitworth who tried to organise his visits to the nearest second. On one occasion he suddenly opened a door on the basement and had a 10-minute chat with the boilerman, who showed him how it all worked. A red-faced Whitworth had to quickly reorganise the timetable. Instead of eating with all the big knobs HRH would choose to have fish & chips with the students. I think he had Whitworth weighed up.

Old Ramage still had a grudge against me and I had to wait 3 months before my grant began. Fortunately, the rapidly growing number of undergraduate courses meant that there was plenty of well-paid teaching work available, especially in the lab, which helped to keep us in bread. He was mortified to discover me one day, living on soup and chips in the refectory, suggesting I bought something more substantial. I reminded him that my grant had still not materialised, and to give him credit he was genuinely sorry. He would bring in items from his allotment occasionally from then on. I remember having to teach General Science & Hygiene to a group of 'Cocoa, Chocolate & Sugar

Confectionary' students, many of whom were half-illiterate!

The research topic that Onkle Hans gave me was a complete none-starter and my reading of the chemical literature suggested that there was no way it would ever work. After 9 months of fruitless attempts and little help from Hans I started to scout around for something related that might work, taking advantage of his going on a month's holiday to try out something of my own. I discovered azide chemistry, an area involving potentially explosive compounds. They were highly reactive and full of unexplored interest. By the time he returned I had some interesting results which opened up a totally new field of activity. I picked up courage to tell him and to my relief he was happy with my efforts – and never again mentioned his abortive previous topic.

My lab was an ancient rather tatty one in the old 1896 building with very Spartan equipment and basic facilities. My lab mate was a larger-than-life Armenian called Zhavan Aryan, always cheerful and a whirlwind in the lab, with lots of things boiling away all at the same time. I had to learn the Armenian for 'shut the door' which was something like 'tore kotse' – but he still left it open. Curiously, many of the useful chemistry journals were on shelves in Ramage's office so one had to knock and ask to consult the items.

Not long after that, the smart new Science and Engineering building was opened. Unfortunately the dear old Principal, Dr Venables, now moved on to higher realms, had visited USA and decided that the future was 110 volts, so all our equipment required transformers and our new equipment had to be USA-style. This complication was exacerbated by a change of mind some months later and the whole building went back to 240 volts – and all our equipment was changed again!

The new labs were brilliant. Hans had his own bench in the lab and still occasionally conducted an experiment, but not for long. Unknown to me, he still hankered after his original idea and decided to utilise my new azide compounds to tackle this. He had no idea of their lethality on heating. One lunchtime he had set up a small flask half full with some brown liquid with a Bunsen burner beneath it and a thermometer in the flask. As he left the lab he said to me 'can you keep an eye on that flask, it should be kept at about 130 degrees'. I went round to look at the flask, just in time to witness an enormous explosion. My lab-coat was spattered with bits, I was totally deaf and the bits of flask, together with the thermometer which behaved like a missile, went straight through the ceiling tiles. Hans stood at the door with a white face, relieved to discover that miraculously, apart from being a little shaken I was all right. He explained to my utter amazement what he had been attempting. He had been heating 30 grams of an undiluted azide, a known explosive. I had to bite my tongue as I revealed his stupidity. He never tried another experiment.

After this stuttering start, research went along well despite the lack of money and facilities. These hard times proved a valuable lesson for later years. I had friends in industry and in USA who ran spectroscopic measurements for me until eventually we bought the equipment. Eventually, I managed to convince Ramage to invest a large sum in new equipment – and send me on courses to use it. He could easily be convinced to sign up for 1000's but would argue vehemently over pence. The department was growing fast and soon the premises for chemistry were bursting at the seams. A brilliant, young, enthusiastic and hard-working bunch of staff were employed and the place was buzzing. Feo Scheinmann, from hostel days, returned from the USA after a post-doctoral spell to join the staff. Many others were taken on including a larger-than-life Analytical chemist, Stuart Bark. The chemistry staff in total grew eventually to over 60.

Soon after getting started on my azide work I found that adding nitrite to an amine I was using in order to make my azide, produced a deep orange colour, even at very low concentrations. I mentioned this to Stuart Bark, thinking it might be a good way of determining low concentrations of nitrite, a common material added to foods as a preservative. Within a couple of months we published a paper on this, still a useful application. My first ever research paper.

I recall taking Harry Locksley, a new Australian staff member, to a conference soon after he had started. He became very agitated when one lecturer was explaining his research on an interesting product derived from ants. Harry whispered 'he's got the structure wrong!' so I urged him to challenge the speaker in the question time, which he did. Harry walked to the front and wrote the correct structure, explaining why – it had been the subject of his Masters research. The flummoxed speaker's only retort was 'you've got the structure upside down' to which Harry replied 'well that's because I'm from the ANTipodes' to howls of laughter and applause. Harry had arrived on the UK scene and continued to publish work on natural products for many years, often in partnership with Feo, including the structure of the components making up ginger and how the flavour changed with their differing proportions.

Back in Blackpool we joined an appallingly awful church of the Brethren, expecting the friendly and earnest spirit we experienced in our last congregation. They were for the most part the most miserable and grim-faced bunch of people we had met in our brief lives together. We tried hard to integrate, even helping dear old Bill

Bargery, one of the only bright lights, run the youth group composed mostly of the local council house kids, who ran fairly wild. On one occasion I convinced a few of the kids to come to an evening service. As the girls trooped in, one old (and miserable) stalwart church member rounded on one of the girls saying 'where's your hat?!' Not surprisingly, they never returned, and we didn't stay too long either. After a spell at the local Baptist church, which again had a strong puritanical streak as well as some good folks, we ended up at a small village church.

In those pre-pill days it was not too surprising that Jean soon became pregnant. The TB doctors were not happy at the news despite Jean being remarkably well, even more so after getting over morning sickness. She was told she would have to return to hospital to have her baby and the child would have to be kept in for several weeks for checks. Slowly, as our minimal finances allowed, we equipped the house with the essentials for living, but they were the bare essentials. In those days before central heating, double glazing and insulation, houses were cold and draughty and our only source of heat was a coal fire in the back room, which itself caused a draught at floor level. Fortunately we had our love to keep us warm.

My fellow research students were a lively bunch. Peter Miles was a brilliant mimic, great linguist and fine chemist, working for Hans. He could take off old Hans, with his soft Austrian accent and Ramage with his Geordie twang to perfection. If Ramage was away, Peter would phone Ramage's secretary, knowing she had the girls in her office drinking tea, and say 'Whatistacallit, I've just popped back to pick up a folder and will be with you in a minute or two'. A flurry of females shot out of the nearby office as we all peered out of the lab door giggling. Another very quiet guy, Bob Higginbottom, had a project to make some unknown compounds called dibenzoxazepines for his MSc. He succeeded with no trouble – that is until he tried to make the parent compound of the series. We all had to evacuate the labs for several days until every trace of the materials he had used was disposed of in an incinerator. This compound was a really potent 'lachrymator' – that is, it made your eyes stream with tears. A couple of months later a couple of chaps in long rain coats and Homburg hats turned up to enquire about this incident. Hans disclosed everything, they took copious notes, but we had no idea who they were – and we never heard more, at least, not for several years. Many years later, when I was on the staff of the now renamed Salford University, I met an American in charge of a grant office for the American Army Research in Europe. I asked him what he did in his research days and he told me of his work on CR gas. It appeared it had been discovered in an English University by accident and was developed by Porton Down. It was, indeed, Higginbottom's lachrymator! When I told him the story he immediately offered me a large post-doctoral grant –'we owe you one' he said. I had this grant for a number of years. Apparently the two Homburg hat men were indeed from Porton Down and despite much research in the UK and USA no better analogue was ever found. CR gas – better known to us as Higginbottom's lachrymator - is still the best riot control substance known to man.

My research blossomed and soon resulted in another paper or two, though Hans was incredibly finicky, slow and almost fearsome to finalise and send off the papers. Jean was quite adept at typing and took on the terrible job of typing up student's theses, with numerous carbon copies, which meant that mistakes had to be corrected on each copy and being highly technical, was altogether a slow process. She earned a useful if tiny pittance for her labours. Hans lent us a 'Moses basket' in which his son had been brought up, and after us, numerous other research students used the same cot.

Our son Mark was born in December of the same year we were married and despite the weeks of monitoring him and Jean, all proved in order, and as if to prove his health, he had an incredibly powerful set of lungs. We spent much of the next 18 months being woken several times a night. I recall we were both feeling very tired one night when I picked him up from his cot, took him into the bare-floored back bedroom in his sleeping bag and lay him on the floor, lying next to him with a couple of blankets and a pillow. He went straight to sleep and a couple of hours later I awoke feeling stiff, and went back to bed; we had our best night's sleep for ages. When we decided to visit Jean's parents we would load up the large Silver Cross pram with everything, walk the mile and a half to the station and get the steam train, repeating the walk of a couple of miles to Chorlton-on-Medlock at the other end. Despite our importunity we were very happy and content.

My grandfather had managed to get a bit more restitution money for me as a lump sum, which proved sufficient to buy a brand new Ford Cortina, which meant I had to pass my driving test – which I achieved second time round. Jean managed it in one go. Life suddenly improved a notch or two. Ramage even engineered a better Studentship for me, so suddenly we were a little better off. We decided that two children were not too much more pain than one and almost two years later Delia turned up. I recall Jean telling me at 4 o'clock one morning that she had started to get regular contractions and maybe we should go to the Maternity Hospital. We arrived not too long after and I left Jean who was giving all her details to the admission nurse. I only discovered when I phoned at 10 o'clock that not only had our daughter been born but that it happened 20 minutes after her arrival! When I visited, Jean was looking sprightly, writing letters and this delightful little peaceful bundle, with a beak nose, looking like a Red Indian, was in the cot next to her. She proved a very well behaved baby and had a dramatic effect on Mark who from then on slept like a hibernating bear. Delia had arrived and, of course, our lives changed again.

My research work continued for three years and I wrote up my thesis and submitted it for the still unknown Research Diploma of the Royal Institute of Chemistry. This was the first in Britain and required me to go down to London to their prestigious headquarters in Burlington House, Piccadilly, where two senior chemistry professors gave me a grilling for a couple of hours about my work and a lot else to see if I was worthy of the honour. One of the profs, John Cadogan, later became a good friend and colleague, and after a spell at Edinburgh University he became chairman of BP and obtained a knighthood.

I duly obtained the diploma in 1961 and was offered a place on the staff of the fast-growing department of chemistry at Salford as an Assistant Lecturer, Grade B, on a salary of £888 pounds per year, a veritable prince's ransom. Many other chemists joined us including Brian Iddon, Basil

Wakefield, Bob Smalley – who was another of Han's research students, Doug Maas, Alan Fitton and John Hill. We were the youngest and one of the largest departments in Britain since we ran courses for London degrees, a final year ARIC course – which proved very popular with industrially based students, as well as two Sandwich courses that ran back-to-back. That is, students spent 6 months in Salford and 6 months in industry. I taught on one of these Sandwich courses. It had the great virtue that I had to visit students in industry to check their progress. In this way I was able to build up good relationships with key people in the chemical industry and quickly took up the 'Tomlinson principle' when offered. You may recall Ken Tomlinson had told me while at Lankro that he furnished his house and paid for holidays by having a second job, in his case writing. I became a consultant at Geigy in Manchester, as it then was. This also soon resulted in a research grant to allow me to take on a PhD student and was the beginning of a long and fruitful relationship both in Manchester and later in Basle, Switzerland.

I recall putting on a workshop at Geigy where I showed them the power of modern methods to solve their chemistry problems, every example being one of their in-house headaches. This proved so effective that they ended up equipping the labs and plant with all the latest methodology that I had outlined. I later conducted similar workshops in Basle and at other companies in Britain. These were chemistry boom years and the academic world had much to offer industry. Another benefit of the Sandwich courses was to bring to light interesting problems from industry that, while not directly relevant to the company, needed investigating. Some resulted in new research projects. On one occasion I returned from Geigy with a puzzle to sort out. Why was one of their starting materials always orange in colour? It should have been white. It made no difference to Geigy since the colour disappeared in downstream chemistry. I was working on it in the lab with a view to give it as an undergraduate project in the final year of the Sandwich course when Hans asked me what I was up to and I explained. I solved the problem showing that the pure material was indeed white but rapidly underwent a reaction with oxygen in the air to give an intriguing by-product, the structure of which I sorted out. A perfect project.

To my amazement the following new term brought a new research student financed by Hans working on this very chemistry for a PhD! He had no discussion with me and not even with Geigy. I was astounded. Unfortunately, this became a regular feature of Hans' dealings with me. He would offer me a joint studentship grant where I ran the project, put in the ideas to get it going, and he would take the credit. He would lecture on 'his' new research and publish papers with his name as the principal author. I was in a quandary as my future was dependent upon his say-so. It took me several years to get out from his old-man-of-the-sea methods that Sinbad suffered from, and strike out on my own. The first time I published Salford work without him named he did not speak to me for months. This maybe was the Austrian system but it certainly did not suit me.

Treading delicately, I was promoted to a full lecturership and not too long after that to a senior lecturer post, Hans needing me more than I needed him. I always acknowledged him in papers, even if he had no part in them and he left me largely to run joint PhD students research, though I would obviously keep him informed. I managed to get grants (and consultancies) from companies such as Monsanto in Ruabon, North Wales and ICI departments in Manchester as well as pockets of money from the College, though with so many staff this was thin on the ground.

Meanwhile the two children grew fast and it was not long before we had to kit out Mark for the local primary school and wave him off in his smart shorts and blazer. The 1963 winter before he began school proved a fierce one. The sea actually froze and mini-icebergs could be seen on Blackpool Beach. For the first time in living memory Stanley Park lake froze over and we with lots of others, took sledges and enjoyed the winter frolics. Our bedroom windows remained totally frozen over – inside – for weeks, with ever thickening ice. Snow lay thick and the children loved it. My commuter train struggled to get through to Manchester and the whole country was semi-paralysed, some areas totally cut off.

Delia was most aggrieved that Mark was off to school but not her. She would pick up a book or paper and, holding it upside down or sideways, pretend to read it. She was always very competitive, her favourite word being 'Me!' when it came to one of them to do something first. Well before starting school, she had some reading ability as well as anything else that Mark would proudly demonstrate from his schooling.

Around this time Jean's mother decided she wanted to sell her Blackpool house and gave us first option to buy it. Mortgages were difficult to obtain and it took some doing to raise one, the house costing the princely sum of £1800. Cap in hand I had to persuade a dubious manager of a minor building society to trust that my slowly growing income would adequately repay the loan. We succeeded and became householders and slowly managed to cover bare floorboards and obtain or make furniture. Jean made most of the children's clothes as well as some of her own and we were a happy home-owning family.

Chapter 9

Nearly Norwegian speaking

Two major changes in the next few years transformed my career. In 1965 I applied for and gained a prestigious post-doctoral post at the University of Oslo in Norway for a year, taking unpaid leave from my Salford job. I was encouraged, especially by Danny White to broaden my research education. The second change was even more dramatic. In 1967 the Royal College of Adv. Tech. became Salford University. (In 1966 I received an invite to speak in the USA. The letter was addressed to me at 'The Royal College of Advertising Techniques'. I stopped abbreviating after this)

We put our house in the hands of an agent and rented it for a year which adequately covered the mortgage. We packed everything into and onto our Ford Cortina, complete with an enormous trunk on the roof and the two children perched on mountains of goods and set off on a cold and blustery January day to travel by ferry from Newcastle to Oslo, a one-and-a-half day trip. The ferry sailed in the evening and we saw an astounding smorgasbord laid out in the ferry dining-room, the tables groaning with every kind of fish and meat, salads and hot dishes. Dinner would be served in the harbour before setting sail. Beautiful linen cloths were laid with finest glasses and tableware. We told the excited children they would have to behave and not spill anything. At that moment a waitress came with a jug of water – and tipped it, *not* into our glasses but onto the tablecloth! Red-faced, we realised the portent of this but the kids just couldn't stop giggling. We enjoyed the dinner but soon were glad of the wet tablecloth stopping our plates sliding about. This proved to be our last meal before we arrived in Oslo harbour. We discovered sea mountaineering. A massive storm raged outside. The engines were either struggling on an upslope or screaming on the down. Although we were not sea-sick, unlike many, we had no interest in food or going out on deck for more than a brief look. Sleeping also eluded us, though the kids were perfectly happy and went to the galley pinching biscuits and other delicacies.

We entered Oslo Fjord and at last had some respite for sleep and the second morning saw us berthed in the harbour, with thick snow, a temperature of -8 degrees outside and a superb breakfast was being served. As we were finishing, a young man came up to our table, shook my hand, bowed and, to my astonishment said 'Bugger'! I was nonplussed and the kids were once more in fits of giggles. He explained in my speechless state that he was Andreas Bugge from the Chemistry Department of Oslo University, and that he had come to escort me to the University residence. He explained that our car would be available on the dockside. We watched in trepidation as our car was not driven but craned high over the ship side, still fully loaded. After brief formalities we all climbed aboard with Andreas in his Saab ahead of us. He shot off, snow flying. Our English car had no snow tyres and I had never driven on snow before.

Fortunately, the heavy load minimised the skidding as we slithered up out of the city towards the famous Holmenkollen ski jump area of Blindern where we had an apartment waiting. It was quite some journey but we made it and disembarked, Mark still in his shorts, as was the norm for English children. The brand new apartment proved brilliant, thoroughly insulated and double- or triple-glazed, warm and well equipped. Central heating meant that we had no idea of outside temperature and a central laundry catered for our larger washing needs while a communal excellent washing machine in the basement handled the rest. We were one of a few post-doctoral families, our neighbours with two similarly aged children, being Japanese. We were all on an excellent grant from the NTNF (Norges Teknisk-Naturkatenskappelige Forschningsrad by name). My Professor was the likable and brilliant Salo Gronowitz, a Swede from Upsala University, recently moved to Oslo. The other recipients were from all over the world. The NTNF decided that the first requirement for us all was to learn how to ski and took us for a week's skiing tuition not far from Lillehammer, up in the mountains. It was marvellous and the kids had a special ski school which they loved. We bought cross-country skis and special small ones for the children. Delia had an endearing habit of always turning to her left down a hill so we would face her well right of the destination and give her a gentle push. Following this introduction, Jean and I would drop the children at school (a private English school, used by embassies and NATO for Mark and a Barnehagen – an outdoor Kindergarten – for Delia) and go from our door on cross-country ski tours. Delia would dress up in an amazing outfit that was incredibly warm and waterproof and the kids would play out whatever the weather. The temperature never went above zero for months in winter so the air was incredibly dry and with Oslo being surrounded by hills, it was rarely windy. I would walk the mile to my laboratory and as long as my ears were covered would enjoy the trip, always in snow. We quickly realised that shorts were totally inappropriate wear for a Norwegian winter! Following a morning off skiing I would work in the evenings to make up for it.

The labs were very well equipped and I had a fine bunch of colleagues around me. Research was on a totally different area of chemistry than I was familiar with, namely Thiophene chemistry. These sulphur-containing compounds were beginning to become important in pharmaceuticals in particular. I was able to introduce new methods from my experience and learn excellent new chemistry and techniques from Salo. Many years later, when I started to publish a series of books called 'Best Synthetic Methods', I persuaded Salo to write one on Thiophenes and it became a big seller in the series.

We joined an American Lutheran church full of NATO and embassy people. It was a very smart and modern building and the folks were a cheerful and very American bunch. I even joined the choir, learning what fine singers Americans were and brilliant harmonisers. We experienced all kinds of American specialities such as Thanksgiving dinners and other very un-English events. We found that food was particularly expensive with meat being both unrecognisable in the butchers and ludicrously expensive. In winter, fruit and vegetables were in short supply and not imported unless absolutely necessary. So we would sometimes eat in the University refectory which was subsidised. They served up a superb, tasty meat stew in rich gravy which we always enjoyed called 'hvallbiff'. It turned out to be whale meat!

Our neighbours as I mentioned were from Japan. Emi Shibata was the mother of two young boys, Kiwamo and Tsukuru, similarly aged to ours. Emi was an English teacher in Japan but her spoken English was hardly understandable. Jean took in hand to teach her to speak Lancastrian, which she rapidly progressed with. Her boys would knock on our door and say, in a squeaky voice, 'Can we come in?' and would play for hours, especially with Lego. They romped about with our two outdoors and we could hear lots of chatter but not understand a word! They learnt some mystical children's means of communicating. After a couple of months, Kiwamo, who went to a Norwegian school, refused to speak anything other than Norwegian at home! Once their quiet and taciturn father discovered Lego – he visited us to find out what the children kept talking about – he bought an enormous set and the children would come up bearing his latest creation; an aeroplane or complex engine, he being an engineer. Our two and their young friends would go through a book together, such as animals, and they would say the English name, to howls of laughter, and would respond similarly to the Japanese. We still can count to ten in Japanese and know that Hana is the Japanese for an elephant's trunk. Also, a climbing frame in

Japanese is a 'JungleJim'. They were delightful kids and we all missed them when they went back home.

Eventually, winter passed and instead of skiing, using maps that went across bogs and lakes, we explored the hills and the seaside places along the Oslo Fjord. In June, we decided to go camping in Hardanger Fjord area and then drive north to an Australian family who lived in Trondheim who we had met in Lillehammer skiing week. It was a lovely holiday though unbelievably cold at night in our little tent. The Ford survived the winter despite its unsuitability in cold weather. I would bring the battery indoors if I needed the car next day and even then would often have to dig the car out or get the snowplough man to tow me to start. On the way north we stopped at the farm of one of my work colleagues in Tynset, far from any town. On arrival we were mystified that the cows in his fields were rushing about and leaping crazily. The farmer, who spoke impeccable English, learnt from the BBC, explained that he had just let them out of their winter barns, it being midsummer's day! We arrived after a long journey in Trondheim at about 930pm and straight away our children and theirs went off into the large grounds to play, while we enjoyed a glass of home-made wine. (It is worth recording that most people made wine from all kinds of fruit. We once visited a spinster colleague from my Chemistry department who lived well out of Oslo near Kongens Utsikt – the Kings View - and she showed us her basement, covered in bubbling carboys of wine, hundreds of litres of it. She probably supplied the whole area. Alcohol was not cheap and only a few government-controlled outlets sold it. Much of the Chemistry Department's absolute alcohol was used to fortify such wine apparently). Back in Trondheim the sun was still high in the sky as we adults ate some delicious fish dish, noting that the time was 1100pm and no sign of the children. They came in around midnight, ravenous, but still in daylight.

Back in Oslo we enjoyed days in the Frogner Park, swimming with the children, eating freshly caught and boiled shrimps straight from the boat in the harbour and often getting a polite notice from the police on our English-number-plated car for parking in the wrong place or going up a one-way street the wrong way. We never had to pay a fine.

The Norwegians still had a great fondness for Brits from the last war, which from their perspective seemed not long ago, given the amount of discussion in the papers and television on the subject. One May day we set off early for Oslo to do some shopping and parked in an empty market square. What we didn't realise was that it was the King's birthday and endless numbers of brass bands collected at this square on their way to the palace. When we got back to the square, there was our car surrounded by dozens of bands getting organised. We sloped off to buy some Småmat (small food, literally, a kind of stew) lunch until things quietened. Norwegians lived well but ate rather a basic diet for the most part. We enjoyed their open sandwich ideas – they had a great word for the stuff one puts on a sandwich – Palegg – which means 'put on'. They had shops that only sold palegg, and their bread was excellent. However, their hot food was fairly uninspiring. Some of their favourite foods left us unimpressed such as fish buried in the ground until it becomes a jelly, dug up and eaten or ancient goat cheese, both stinking awful. Most of these delicacies are ancient peasant methods for preserving foods. In Britain we have similar foods such as haggis and Lancashire hotpot.

Delia joined Mark at the excellent English school and was in her element. She made plenty of friends and a regular feature was the arrival of a chauffeur-driven limousine arriving at our apartment to take her to an embassy party. Jean decided to try to learn Norwegian and I joined her in the attempt. We were always thwarted by the excellent English, even of the young children. We would stop somewhere and ask the way in our best Norsk to be enthusiastically greeted in English. Norwegian is more a song than a spoken language and that is a contributory factor. Learning the tune is an integral part of conversing. They have some delightful customs and dozens of ways of saying thanks. If you meet someone you haven't seen for months or years you say 'Takk for sist' which means 'Thanks for the last time', even if the last time was 50 years ago.

On one occasion, following a Scandinavian Chemical Congress, I attended the Viking-style dinner that ended the event. Food is brought round comprising of plentiful, very tasty lean meat (I asked my Norwegian neighbour what kind of meat it was. He did not know the English but mimed the animal. Ah, I said, Moose, which brought gales of laughter. Moose is Norwegian for mouse). Then someone gives a speech with much laughter and little meaning to me, followed by more meat etc. This eating and speeching continues until no one can eat any more, lubricated with copious alcohol, of course. We ate Moose, Reindeer and several other such venisons.

During my stay the Nobel prize was awarded to one of the world's finest organic chemists ever, an American named Robert Burns Woodward. He was a chain-smoking and heavy drinking genius and it was the custom that the Norwegians wrote a biography of the Laureate. They could find no one intrepid enough to take on the task and pleaded with me to do it. Carefree and undaunted I took up the challenge, which fortunately fitted the bill, including an appropriate photograph of him in his lab smoking while handling the highly inflammable solvent, ether.

My research work progressed well and despite Salo moving back to Sweden late in my stay we published several papers together and Jean and I spent an enjoyable spell in Lund where he took up a post as Professor at the University, driving the 400 miles in snow with chains on the tyres of our faithful chariot. In those days Sweden still drove on the left, as in UK, which meant we had to change over on a border bridge, supposedly following the lane marking. Unfortunately the markings were under a couple of feet of snow but somehow we managed it unscathed.

We returned to Newcastle on a much quieter ferry in January 1966, with the Oslo temperature at -4 while Newcastle was +4 degrees, grey and perishing. The damp air made it feel so much colder and we were all a bit depressed. We set off back to our home in Blackpool hardly speaking, and though none of us felt hungry we stopped at a pub in Yorkshire for a change of scene. The blazing log fire, lovely cheerful people and good English food and beer, with the first beef we had eaten for a year sent us on our way feeling much better and glad to be home.

Within a day of re-starting their schooling, Mark and Delia had dropped their rather upper-crust

English and returned to speaking Lancastrian, much to our amazement but no doubt at the cost of much ribbing from their friends.

Chapter 10

Nearly converted to Norwegian living

We arrived at our cold, draughty house, with its coal fire, no central heating and leaky, single-glazed windows, appalled at how bad the design of British houses were compared to Scandinavian ones. We decided right away to replace our coal fire with gas to eliminate a major source of draughts and install secondary glazing, a cheaper compromise than the superb window and door construction in Norway. I went round the house trying to improve the leaks and draughty aspects, front and back. Slowly we invested in carpeting and made our property as sensible and snug as we could, given our limited means. It still felt chilly and less cosy than we had hoped. The new University status that came along not too long after our return meant a healthy pay rise as we were transferred onto University pay scales and we decided that a move was the best way forward. My very early morning commute could be shortened if we moved to Kirkham, still on the main Manchester line with more train options as well. Jean and the children would still live in a healthy atmosphere compared to smoky greater Manchester. We actually looked at some of the small towns around Manchester but the dank, foreboding stone houses of ex-mill towns, the smoke-blackened residences and very busy roads completely turned us off the idea.

So it was that we moved to the pleasant town of Kirkham, made famous by Lowry's 'A Lancashire village' painting, with a good school a mere 50 yards from our house on Wyre Avenue and a short bike ride to the station. The house we bought was twice the price of our first one, built on a hill side but generally much better suited to our family requirements. At first the mortgage payments were painful but inflation soon lessened the pain. We had fine neighbours, nearby a good village of shops and market, a nearby swimming pool, where Mark and Delia learnt to swim at a good level of proficiency and a pleasant, small village church in nearby Inskip. Again, no coal fire and secondary glazing improved the warmth and insulation and fully carpeted rooms made for a snug winter residence. Not quite Norwegian standards but getting there slowly.

On returning to Salford and taking up my position on the staff again I had a new string to my bow on the research front – thiophenes. This was a Suschitzky-free zone. Brian Iddon had worked in a related area and told me of a company, MYTD (Midland Yorkshire Tar Distillers), which made thiophene. Contacting them they sent me a gallon can of thiophene as well as samples of other gems. What a find! They also asked me to come down and give them a talk about my work. This was the beginning of a long and fruitful relationship for me and for them.

When cheap and plentiful North Sea gas came on stream, coal gas disappeared. This meant that industries that made the gas by heating coal all but packed up. They were dotted throughout Britain and were often little changed from Victorian times. After removal of the gas, coal tar was then produced from the residue and finally it left coke, an important fuel. Coal tar was a source of many important and useful chemicals such as phenols, naphthalenes, pyridines and thiophenes, all vital for making drugs, dyestuffs, plastics and numerous other key compounds. MYTD had a young and enthusiastic staff determined to replace coal tar with North Sea gas or petroleum as the feedstock for making these chemicals and asked me if I would join them in this exciting venture as a consultant. They would also give me a grant to conduct thiophenes research to help put them on the map. Within a couple of years we became the world's major supplier of thiophenes, pushing the market leaders in USA out of the market and built up a highly successful business. My chief colleague down there was a young man of great flair and dynamism, Rex Clark, who had come up through the ARIC course just like me. We remained friends and colleagues throughout our careers and still are friends and near neighbours today, almost 50 years on.

Chapter 11

Nearly no longer nearly

Although I was able to put Res Dip RIC after my name, it did not quite have the ring of PhD and being 'Mr' rather than Doctor definitely had a second division feel in academic circles. Now that Salford could give its own degrees and doctorates I decided to write up yet another thesis, which Jean typed, for the first ever PhD presented by Salford University. It had to be solely my own work but this presented no problems. I had always kept an active bench going on my own and some of my Norway work could also be included. So at the first degree ceremony of the new University I at last could honestly be called doctor, not 'nearly doctor'. Curiously, no such problem existed during my stay in Norway where my title was always doctor, having done the appropriate work to earn it.

The new University status brought another wave of new appointments, including my upgrade to senior lecturer, with a number of new external and internal professorships being created, one of whom was Hans. Two more chemistry professors from Wales also arrived with their staff colleagues and research students, Profs Orville-Thomas and Glyn Phillips. The former of the two became Head of Department and had a low view of the existing staff, announcing that there would be no new advancements without the candidates having a DSc. This Doctorate of Science is a prestigious award based on a large body of research publications of significance. Hans had just achieved this. We discovered that as a young man in a small community in Wales, the Head was called Orville Thomas but decided that the double-barrelled name had more prestige. He proved to be the most pompous twerp ever appointed at Salford. Like Mussolini, he was small and tended to strut around showing his importance. He would begin a course of lectures to students with the preface 'These lectures will certainly be the finest you will ever hear'. I recall on one occasion he called me down to his office and his opening remark was 'Meth-Cohn, you are the most selfish chemist I have ever met!' I was dumbfounded, having no clue as to what caused the outburst. It turned out that he and I had independently applied to the Science Research

Council for a grant to buy new NMR equipment (the modern analogue in hospitals is the MRI scanner; ours was for solving structural problems; Orville's was for pure research). Apparently my application was successful and his was not. I was briefly the toast of the department, especially since the award had not yet been officially announced. Several of my friends and colleagues did indeed get their DSc degrees. Nine years after my PhD award, I also obtained the first ever University of Salford DSc. I think Orville had a growing respect for the abilities of his Organic Chemistry colleagues in the interim, as his output declined and ours grew rapidly. We became the largest Chemistry Department in Britain, maybe in Europe and produced a tenth of all chemists going into industry in the UK.

On one occasion, I had been invited to lecture at Imperial College, the Prof being Sir Derek Barton, Nobel Prize winner. This was one of the key Chemistry Departments in the country and I had experienced him tearing a speaker to shreds if they made any error in a conference address. I went down there in some fear. Fortunately the monthly Chemistry Journal of the Royal Society of

Chemistry had just appeared, containing eleven papers from Salford, three being mine. He introduced me, clutching this Journal, and telling his colleagues and students what an impressive place Salford was and they should do likewise. I gave my lecture and to my relief he made a number of really useful suggestions to continue the work. We became good friends from then on and later even published together. Phew!

It was decided that Salford needed more space for its burgeoning chemistry department and a new ten storey building would be erected. Unfortunately, we came at the end of a spate of new building projects in the Universities, which meant that we received a limited budget to achieve our goals. The new Department was built on a shoestring with awful, single-glazed windows and much second-rate facilities but at least we had space. The opening of the new block was made by Prince Philip our Chancellor and he was intrigued by the new pair of Paternoster lifts. These were two-person cubicles that ran permanently with no door. He asked for a demonstration and questioned what happened when it went below ground – did it invert, he asked with a grin? Two volunteer students entered the lift and while below ground stood on their hands, much to the pleasure of HRH but not to the red-faced Vice-Chancellor. These proved a boon to most users but the occasional visitor came a cropper. One visiting painter tried to take his step-ladder up the lift and succeeded in bending both his ladder and the cubicle. Today, Elf & Safety no longer allow such useful devices, sadly. There was an ordinary lift for the unsure. My office was on the sixth floor and I chose to walk mostly unless I was in a hurry.

Finally, I seemed to have arrived, 'nearly' no longer. There is much yet to say but it will have to be under another title. Maybe 'The what if man'.

Epilogue

You may reasonably wonder how I discovered all the tales I have described herein. It was a long and slow process.

Much of the information regarding my mother and her background and the family came from discussions with family and friends of my mother and of her parents. In 2002, I took my son and daughter to visit all the places linked to my mother's background and my upbringing in southern Germany. In Schwäbisch Gmünd we met a lovely soul, Ortrud Seidel who had lived in the town all her life. She knew my family and well remembered my grandparents and their store, as well as my mother. She wrote a book – 'Mut zur Errinnerung' (Courage to remember) in German, in which she described the lives of all the Jews of the town who were murdered by the Nazis. It was good to get first-hand knowledge from her. Similar meetings with children I had lived with in Herrlingen, various archive authorities and people my mother had lived with or been friends of were really useful. The numerous letters written by my mother in her hard-to-read and often rushed, old

Germanic script were collected by her sister Hertl and came to me via her son, the famous war photographer, Micha Bar Am. There is still much we do not know. Despite much effort I still know nothing much about my father. I can only imagine that he died in the war as a German soldier.

There is a suggestion that my mother went from The Hague firstly to Sweden, where a good friend was living and working in a remarkable organisation supporting woman, still in existence today. Despite some effort I have not been able to substantiate this.

My sojourn with the Ware family has left an indelible impression on me and on my lifestyle. I only realised the extent of this when I renewed contact with them after more than 60 years. My only link, apart from a few vague memories, was an address in Edinburgh on my Naturalisation papers. Jean and I visited the address, having firstly made contact with a very helpful lady who lived a couple of houses down from us on Upper Dean Terrace. Through her we discovered sufficient to make the internet search for the Ware children possible. I firstly Googled Harry

Fabian Ware, discovering, to my amazement that he was the son of the famous Sir Fabian Ware who created the Commonwealth War Graves Commission. I found one website of a professional artist who had been taught by Harry after the war in Malvern. Through him I discovered that Charlie Ware was alive and active, running the world centre for Morris Minor spare parts, based in Bath! One evening, making marmalade, the phone rang – it was Charlie! My marmalade was burnt but the call was worth it. The following evening I was making marmalade again, having thrown out the first batch. When the phone rang again I switched off the heating of the marmalade, answered the phone and it was Gill. We arranged a get-together. My only sadness was that I had not reached them earlier. Armyne had lived to be 100 years old and often wondered what had become of me.

Sadly, Charlie died this year after a long illness and Gill is now living in California. However, we had one last grand reunion, together with Charlie's children, at the unveiling of a Blue Plaque in London to commemorate Sir Fabian having lived there. It turned out to be a fitting send-off to my old playmate and now friend. Charlie had been a remarkable character in Bath, having, unwittingly, become a millionaire in buying up and restoring Bath Georgian houses, rather than allowing the council to pull them down and replace with modern inferior properties. He was a great preserver, loving all things old.

The Ware diary records and photographs came via Gill and of course, much reminiscing filled in many gaps. The final letter from Harry to the National Childrens' Home was amongst the other revealing literature that came from the NCH when I asked them for any information regarding my stay in the orphanage. Some of the news was surprising, to say the least!

I often wondered how I knew the names of lots of wild plants, birds and the like, why I enjoyed scrumping for wild foods, what led me into painting after I retired, how I took to looking after myself from my teenage years with little effort. All these are down to the Ware's upbringing and I am for ever grateful to them, even if it was such a brief stay. Even marmalade making is probably down to the Ware lifestyle.

Amongst other mementos of my past, Gill sent me the actual smock that my mother had made, in which I had travelled to Britain! After I outgrew it she wore it, then her teddy and finally her daughter, followed by her daughters teddy and it is still in remarkable condition.

14920517R00131

Printed in Great Britain
by Amazon.co.uk, Ltd.,
Marston Gate.